Teddy Orloff and the Three Onions:

A Cooking Spiel

Table of News Inside

For Sandra Feen
for her lifelong friendship and support

Teddy Orloff and the Three Onions
Book 1
Scene 1
Fevered Latke Thrill, 1946

I

Before the sun could squeeze a little light, Teddy laid out a chipped saucer,
And, with cracked fingernails, tapped Humperdinck about its imperfections:
"It betters the morning to mutter Hansel und Gretel's evening prayers,
though I lack tune, places for pitch, struggle for pious inflections,"
Mused the pastry baker.
"Prepare for days to fly for perfect creamed horns, strangely enough,"
came a recipe," Teddy recited imperfectly.
"Tread from full moon till the cover of an empty sky.
It's a puff that's needed, A precise, perfect, flaky puff."

II

A Sunbeam bread truck grinded its way down Parsons Avenue,
And on doors papered fliers of the fever flapped high by its breeze:
"This card for sugar, this card for juice. Line ten cards for lard!
Then Blend! Blend! Blend! Mounds of a creamy cheese,"
Said Teddy at a table with recipe cards.
"Then Bake! Bake! Bake! But to what degree? Oh, quickly goes the night,"
Said the baker, rubbing his head – beading, sparkling.
"No hair to lose over these sweet fixings, no hair to spare.
Baker Resch wants it all learned by rote or route, a bread maker's rite."

III

A fog lifted off melting ice as the truck whined in the darkness,
And the baker finished wiping his pale, moonscape scalp:
"Three hours, I will show Resch my impeccable pastry gravitas.
though these I feel I swim the ocean naked, blanketed only by kelp,"
Said the baker, veins seeping with stress.
"Oh, the revolutions since I bid the old Mud-Waddlers state farewell in '29,"
Continued the worried fellow.
"The Nu is followed by the Nu followed by the Nu followed by...
Yet even so with five down with the fever, who am I to whine?"

Health Department flyers flickered on Parsons apartment doors,
And Teddy carefully memorized monumental measures of lard:
"Our poor five wake with scarlatina painted about faces, limbs, neck.
Their strawberry-bulb tongues over Captain Marvel joke 'send rhubarb,'"
Mumbled Teddy with his first smirk of the day.
"Pie for the sick! Pie for the sick! These days a baker's sales dream,"
Mumbled Teddy, with an atonal aesthete.
"But no sweet pie will cure my sweets of their brash rash.
A confection for the infection would act as well as sour cream."

A heavy door off to the left of the kitchen opened with a creek,
And five red-streaked faces meekly, painfully emerged:
"Oh, how your faces flush like a ring of a sabbath bowl of borscht,
brave hearts each while everyone suffers the scourge,"
Said the father to five peaked faces peaking.
"So nu? So nu? So nu all my pretty babka babies,"
Said the father delicately to his children.
"Have any rashes ceased? Have any fevers waivered,"
so all can run the block again like busy honey bees?"

Five tiny hands rubbed five elbows, red streaks inflamed,
And, followed by five more, caused five mouths to wince, eyes to tear:
"Fines, Dad! Fines! They've said to ask for hundreds with fines.
The old man is here! You should not be here. The old man is here,"
Whispered the oldest to the youngest in singsong rounds.
"Lucia, Mar, Gin, Dorr, Jerzy, try hard not to touch stricken joints,"
Suggested Teddy to his children with dulcet tones.
"Perhaps a hot slab of oatmeal or cod liver oil to soothe.
Perhaps we'll soon see an end to your pain, your heartbreaking moans."

'Do not Enter,' in fact, was the notice 'Per order Board of Health,'
A sign that for days worried the likes of Lucia, Mar, Gin, Dorr, Jerzy:
"So Dad! So Dad! So Dad… What's a fine… what's a contagion?

Say Dad! What's a liable? Did you know Sidney Spiegel has scurvy?"
So shouted the five, knowing their father had been banned from the house.
"What time is it? What's a time when a contagion is through? Aren't you sleepy?"
Continued the rambunctious crowd.
"What's a rash really? Why is it red? How about a good glass of water, cold?
You drink too much, Jerzy. You'll never be able to sleep. Jerzy has to pee-pee."

VIII

Wrapped in a turquoise night coat, Teddy's wife Lila appeared,
And held one eye lid high with a finger, a tear blurring her view:
"Morning rises again, Teddy. The quarantine police shall prowl.
So Papas need hide away as much as that makes my heart beat blue,"
Said Lila, shewing the ailing brood back to bed.
"Off to sleep until darkness abides what morning softly claims,"
Urged the mother to all five.
"Latkes, sheyne Kinder… later, in darkness, when your father returns,
we'll grate potatoes (great)… fry pancakes divine in gurgling oil by flame."

IX

The children stumbled away as Jerzy lastly exited improvising a fart,
And Lila stepped over, patting her worried husband's balding head:
"Your magnificent dome reminds me of the need for an onion, Teddy.
A special one, Teddy. Neither shallot nor chive will work in its stead,"
Said Lila in a whisper, concerned one should learn their broken quarantine.
"Teddy, this savory bulb gleams like a jewel, but finer than alabaster,"
Continued Lila, with a mist in her eye.
"A grand bulb, gifting the right spice – driving scoundrel scarlatina afar…
bolder than the fabulous Hope, purer than any Saucy Stone held by Astor."

X

Sleet pelted the Orloff window overlooking an increasingly busy Parsons Avenue,
And Teddy's chest burned with worry. He fumbled over his dog-eared cards:
"How to find the perfect onion when face to face a looming cream horns test.

Can an onion be as clear as the sleet that riddles protective glass, shard by shard,"
Wondered the baker, pulling a worn coat once worn by another father.
"Teddy, there stands an odd man on our corner, his head rugged like earth,"
Chimed in Lila, helping Teddy rumble arms through ragged sleeves.
"He is gawking, scratching, rubbing his eyes where there appear no tears.
Oh, how the desperate sun radiates his orangish head. Such gleam! Such girth…"

XI

Both Orloffs spied a considerable figure catching drops of the sleet,
And, with extended tongue, licked icicles from cavernous nostrils:
"Teddy, what beast do we now have for a neighborly wanderer?
What monstrous creature stands here devouring Heaven's frozen hostile?"
Queried Lila, finding the morning growing beyond brazen.
"From his melted orange complexion, I suppose ice takes a special flavor."
Shot back Teddy, feeling a desperate need to be wry.
"In days of plague and fathers forced to live isolated from children
Even a wandering Golem deserves a frozen cocktail to savor."

XII

Ice tapped at the window like a Krupa gone wild for good men everywhere,
And, hearing of a Golem, Lila relished not much has changed since the Shtetl:
"Had not city gonifs barred guests, I'd invite this frosted monster up for tea.
Had not these shysters stolen daily greetings, I would put up the kettle,"
Remarked Lila, helping Teddy with his coat.
"Don't slide about ice as best as you may! Show Herr Resch your baker's éclat,"
Advised his sweetheart, while both struggled with sleeves.
"Here's your right sleeve – watch cascading winter hail – enter… oh so gently.
Here's your left sleeve – watch cascading dogmata – wear your scarf, your hat."

XIII

The parents wrestled with the coat as if it were one of their young offsprings,
And for a finishing touch, Lila reached to wrap a scarf about Teddy's neck:
"Oh dear, Teddy, our work's lost; your coat hangs about you inside out.

Scrap this dressing; one cannot be sent after an onion dressed like a hectic wreck,"
Said Lila, pulling the coat over her husband's bewildered head.
"My face has vanished in the wool. Lila you've pulled the wool over my eyes,"
Shouted Teddy, completely submerged in his coat.
"By your fingertips coach the coat, cull this fashion so buttons appear outside.
I know, from winter days passed, this mackinaw remains the perfect size."

XIV

More struggles found Teddy's mack wrapped about his waist like a wool loin cloth,
And with the coat slithering down, the couple flush blushed like overanxious teens:
"Say Lila, like Cabbalistic scholar I've readied my cream horn exhibition.
Say, Lila, by this lip-smacking wrestling let's find sweet ways to break quarantine,"
Said a winking Teddy, a herringbone mackinaw crushed at his feet.
"Dear Teddy! Sweet Teddy! There will be soon good time for a delicious nuzzle,"
Sighed Lila, her face flush for longing.
"First, find the onion. Normally, we'd have kisses before onions, Teddy! Kisses before onions.
Now onions first! Onions then kisses! Onions then whatever one wishes.
Such an odd puzzle."

XV

Lila rearranged Teddy's mack, collars in place, all buttons straightly fastened,
And the couple said their farewells as Teddy stepped toward a frozen deluge:
"Beware the knives of ice, songful rats... beware shyster shiitake salesman.
"Beware the depths some may go. Trust your heart in the face of any dishonest fugue,"
Warned Lila, with a quick peck on Teddy's nose.
"To find the exceptional onion, Teddy, seek Burble Friedel. He's your Virgil, your guide,"
Said, Lila, ushering the stuffed baker into the hall.
"It's that spectacular market you seek. Select the finest glowing onion bulbs three.
But should the Knives of Ice grow thick, oh Teddy, don't be afraid to hide."

I

Teddy stepped into the slick street, hearing the gurgling of his stomach,
And so dreamed passing under the windmill of Mills Café for eggs galore:
"Oh, to pass by its spinning blades and to settle by fork, knife, and mural.
But it's Burble Friedel I need to find, to show the way to the proper onion store,"
Mused Teddy, adjusting his worn fedora.
"So, wind at my brow, ice upon my fedora... but what gold rests in my pocket?"
Said Teddy, pleasantly surprised.
"Oh if such forethought could be a Monday, Tuesday, Wednesday tradition.
Lila has left gold with a hole, dressed in poppies, bread perfect for my lunch docket."

II

Ice sculped milky tombs over mailboxes, bus stops signs, fresh puppy droppings,
And Teddy admired his found bagel in the midst of was once a concrete Earth:
"With such a new wilderness now about me, I'll need to mark my way.
What's good for handsome Hansel should work for Teddy, given my failing mirth,"
Remarked a terrified baker, cheeks burning red.
"Here are careful steps for a difference, careful lest there a discourteous ice skid,"
 Said the baker, dropping pieces of bread to mark his road past.
"A taste for Lu, a smidge for Mar... a little nibble for me... Nosh! Nosh! Nosh!
A wedge for Gin... select portion for Dorr... sliver for Jerzy... uh, two slivers for the kid."

III

Teddy delicately marked his passage with bagel, forgetting his urgent mission,
And, when possible, he helped himself to the pieces most plentiful with poppy:
"My five seem so suddenly far in the past. Ice... there piles ice upon ice.

Poles for power shape as hulks... signs like hanged devils... What of that jalopy?"
Said Teddy, amazed at the plastered world about him.
"We've a frozen Pompeii... though I know of no explosive peak that spews volcanic ice bricks,"
Continued Teddy, sliding across the street while hearing an odd chant.
"You left the hill for a thrill/ YOU'RE RIGHT/ To give life a little whirl/ YOU'RE RIGHT!/
Sound off!/One! Two!/Sound Off!/One, two, three, four, five, six... FIVE, SIX!"

IV

From around a mailbox glacier, Teddy spied a column of chanting ants,
And marveled how they marched towards his bagel trail with antennae fluttering ticks:
"Your Mama's got an auntie face!/SO CUTE!/ She's pincers full of Fury & Grace/SO OUCH!/
Sound off!/One! Two!/SOUND OFF!/One, two, three, four, five, six... FIVE, SIX!"
Came the Ant Column's cadence.
"We are Pismire's Ice Ant Brigade, heading full steam down Pismire's Path,"
Said a lieutenant ant to Teddy.
"Ant Lieutenant Jody, the subject of epic and ant song, reporting, sir wanderer.
We're marching, on this wicked winter's day, to displace Hunger's wrath."

V

For a better view, Teddy cautiously shuffled towards the column.
And, bending low, placed his palms upon the knees of his frosted pants:
"From whence does such a column arrive? To where might you venture to?
Army Ants? December Army Ants? Do I see December Army Ants?"
Said Teddy, unaware that part of the column had carried off his bagel trail.
"Holy mackerel, chrome dome! You're cooking with gas, schnook. What a find,"
Said one ant soldier after another.
"Killer Diller! Look at these bagel remains. What no lox, bud? Salt for the munching.
Army Ants? Not Army Ants... We're Ice Ants, though the uncles we've left behind."

Teddy scuttled closer to the column, seeking worldly advise from this food unit,
And, shivering, asked of Burble Friedel and might DiMaggio play another season:
"So nu, knights, why might Ice Ants be on such a quest, on such an insipid day?
Sweets for the colony, I see. Yet, a grand onion for glorious latkes stands to reason,"
Said, Teddy shivering from exposure.
"Your query need be addressed by a higher rank, for we march in old Pismire's path,"
Said Jody to the quivering baker.
"In truth, your words bear no meaning, shaky man. Herein lies the trouble with ants.
We march as thousands, thousand, thousand ants, should you check your math."

Teddy thought to count towards the exact number of soldiers present,
And, taking careful consideration of the cold, decided such accounting superfluous:
"From a baker's soul in query, who ever witnessed such an icing of the Earth?
Upon such frosting, how are ants marching, on Hannukah… this we can discuss."
Said the baker, proud of his sweet metaphors.
"It's a miracle. It's a miracle seen solely through Ohio's stone-grey light,"
Came a tiny but staccato voice.
"Oh, what a Grand Onion might I have in store for you, brave bald knight, Sir Lance."
Our frigid quest is for the colony; therein lies the trouble with ants, an ant's lot, our rite."

An extremely dignified ant stepped forward, a bright red Busby upon his regal head,
And as he spoke, the column stood at ant attention, a thousand times six feet stomping:

"Oh Captain, my captain, looking as strained as Lincoln in his stone chair,
The trouble with ants… they march never touching the souls of busy traffic romping,"
Said the commander arthropod.
"These fellows march in Pismire's path. Old, decrepit Pismire. Old, fart, tart Pismire,"
Said the officer, removing his head covering.
"Hot diggity dog, schnook; spark your bright beacon, that bulb upon your shoulders.
Ants know onion whereabouts solely for ant tables…. advice from an insect sear."

IX

Teddy bowed his head, glared at the sheerness of the ice, considered all things harsh,
And, while worried of cream horn expositions… of the ants on ice he could only admire:
"Say, crusty Colonel Ant, how might you make nasty utterances of one whom all march?
With such colony chutzpah, why you then say such biting remarks of the ant Pismire,"
Asked the baker, feeling all the more numb.
"Why, he's Commendatore Pismire! With ant mantles come acerbic notes to fear,"
Said the candid insect, wise beyond his height.
"As the Bard himself was wont to say, Pismire, Piss Ant, 'Bull Pizzle,' buggy 'bow case.'
These loving words I say of the boss ant, for I am, indeed, Commendatore Pismire."

X

At that moment… at that instant that Pismire revealed himself, all ants stopped,
And, each to their greatest ability, held up bits of bagel, called out:
"Huzzah! Huzzah! Nuggets for Noshes! Nuggets for Noshes! Long live Pismire!
Under his divine guidance it will be bialys nightly; there's absolutely no doubt,"
Thundered thousands of boisterous insects.

"Ah, such a delectable cacophony of spirit, step your peds for the night's
show,"
Said Commendatore Pismire.
"Please welcome, from the frozen hills of Beck Street, an incomparable ice
artist,
The Sonia Heine of the Ant world, Ms. Rem Brr-Ant and her ice-skating beau!"

XI

More heaven bound 'Huzzahs' whooshed as two skaters zipped through the
baker's legs,
And they shined – adorned in blue crepe paper, tin foil tiaras from a
Thanksgiving parade:
"Imagine, if you will, these divine athletes skate to Beethoven's 6th
Symphony.
Hum fellows hum the Andante as they move. Hum like nightingales in colony
serenade,"
Said Pismire, standing on four legs, waving tempi with two up high.
"Here, there seems only iced concrete but nary a blossom or a leaf green,"
Lamented the Commendatore.
"We've skaters, we've the charity of bagels, yet how to slip them into an ant
hill hole.
But with a Beethoven blessing by hums, our colony's morale remain on the
mien."

XII

Miraculously, Ms. Rem Brr-Ant, with beau in tow, ended their routine with a
triple axel,
And, after ten legs rotated skyward to appear as thirty, Pismire introduced a
second act:
"Now to tickle the cockles of your spiracles, here's a breath of fresh insect
Shakespeare,
Direct from performances of 'A Winter's Bobamayse' at the Globe Theater, Sir
Irving Ant,"
Announced Pismire to a magnificent mandibles applause.
"Oh, to warm a thorax in such cold, but an aria from A Carpenter Ant of
Venice."
Recited the thespian from top of a phone booth.
"Hath not an ant antennae? Do we not desire similar morsels, crunched by
heavy weight,

heated by the sun, chilled by the wind, much like a biped is? Are not size 16
shoes a menace?"

XIII

Irving extended into his best pose as Rem Brr-Ant & Beau skidded into
mailbox legs,
And cries of "Huzzah" along with some empathetic 'OYs' filled the morning
air:
"If you step on us do we not squish? If you tell us a good joke, do we not
guffaw?
And if you 'poison us... uh... should one slaughter us... exterminate... us...
hair..."
Said Irving to a now solemn crowd, pulling a strand of substance from his
mouth.
"If you poison us, then the promise of spring for all fades into iniquity for
infinity,"
Interrupted Pismire's usually calming voice.
"The time has come for all Ice Ants to gather up frozen bagel, to fall into
place.
Hold your mandibles high, fellows! Sense the world as yours! March on in
sanguinity!"

XIV

New columns formed as sleet fell more fiercely, shaping fur iced balls on
Busbies,
And Pismire stood ahead of the column's set to take the brigade out the
winter raw:
"Troops! Let's settle the Queen in an iron-clad post box, away from days of
iciness.
A warm mailbox house, we'll huddle within waiting, patiently, for a spring
thaw,"
Announced Pismire as the ants began a new march.
"But what of Burble Friedel? It is through old Friedel that I might find the
right onion,"
Called out a flustered Teddy to a shouting, insulting crowd of ants.
"The Queen's got six sexy legs! YOU'RE RIGHT! She queens day and night!
Sound off!
One two! Sound off! One two three four five six! FIVE SIX! 'I've got blisters on
my bunion.'"

Watching the column head off into the mist, Teddy felt a slight tug at his ear lobe,
And turning his neck found Jody shouting to get the baker's undivided attention:
"Master Cream Horn, you're new to this world. The onion you seek… it's in the Mix!
Seek out waitress Gretel. She hobbles daily, her head twisted towards that very direction,"
Advised Jody, icicles forming on his mandibles.
"Surely as ants are vulnerable on ice, Gretel shuffles with plates of eggs for the ages,"
Said Jody, shielding himself from the wind with Teddy's lobe.
"She ushers daily at Mills, welcomes no 'Whiner sans a Vintner,' loves her merlot.
Know her by a slashing, gray braid; she shrinks daily, much like her minimalist wages."

I

Finishing his advice to the baker, Jody stepped away from the frozen lobe,
And, with a brewing, exacting gust, the lieutenant ant flew to join his
associates:
"Farewell Soldier Ant! May your journeys bring you the best of morsels.
Be sure to brush after every found meal, lest your tiny teeth be in dire
straits,"
Said Teddy, his smile shrinking since he just received guidance from an ant.
"The road to Herr Resch's bakery appears iced. Earth's glaze rivals all cakes."
Said Teddy admiring the craft of wind and ice.
"Broad Street lights glow like red fondant with ice stalactites. orbs like
dragees.
Do I see Marzipan about the gutters, marble waves better than Resch could
bake?"

II

Teddy began a long shuffle to the Mills Café, reaching in pockets for stray
bialys,
And, with the exception of a number of pesky poppy seeds, he gathered only
lint:
"Odd to find streets so bare... Washington, Cleveland... watch for Cossack
mishigas.
I shall count fantasy Mary Lee Candies caramels consumed, my paunch I take
as hint,"
Said Teddy to himself, navigating an upward slope of rare mid-Ohio hill.
"Such slopes on the path to Burble Friedel should be simpler by neighborly
frills,"
Continued the baker considering significant landmarks.
"Not a diner at the Red Ox or a toke at United Cigars... only ice on Broad.
Certainly, Manager Orr shall look specially that there be light at the Mills."

III

In an alley far past Washington, Teddy heard metal crash about bricked walls,
And a trash can lid rolled into the open, twirling like a top perfectly spun:

"On paths like ombré about a cake, I see yet blurs by bricks red by cans'
silver...
Flashing blurs of grey as if an iced creature found three spots in one for fun,"
Said Teddy moving in for a closer look.
"Now I feel a rub... yes there goes a rub... an ankle... another for another
ankle,"
Said the baker, far more concerned than when chatting with ants.
"I see ice to scrape off the cuff but no living thing that rubbed me, thank
God.
Speaking off the cuff, it's wind determined to alarm, a gust far too eager to
rankle."

IV

Ohio skies lean more often to the grey, this being the case whether it be June
or January,
And Teddy, unsure of every sighting, swore he spotted, in various spots,
greyish cats:
"Ice visions! Phantasms in deliria! Mirages on frozen desert! Ice cream
fantasies!
Yes! That would be best... Ice cream fantasies. Now vibrations... legs... is
that Herr Katz?"
Said Teddy, certain he spotted a fellow baker stumbling though sleet.
"Head another way, Teddy. Herr Resch has closed his doors, rather they are
ice sealed,"
Said Herr Katz, clutching at his fedora.
"His kitchen's barred, his mixers, pipes, spatulas, spoons whisked into
darkness.
Head away. Cream Horn masters will have to wait for what your wisdom shall
reveal."

V

Lumbering, hacking, Herr Katz turned up Fourth disappearing into a storm
squeeze,
And Teddy gripped a corner of the Seneca Hotel against a Broad Street wind
blow:
"My feet are lifting... I float a horizontal, flying baker; the feeling's rather
splendid.

Say, I see the grand Memorial Hall, where Valentino danced, singing "El Relicario,"
Marveled the uplifted fellow.
"Look how high my little toes go. Weeehee! I'm Valentino in grand jeté,"
Shouted Teddy into the blasting wind.
"I would have loved to see him. The Sheik himself, marvelous with the Mineralava,
Lighting up crowds... delightful light... divine light... oh wind whipped... fouetté."

VI

A blast of wind forced Teddy to lose his grip just as a banner ripped from the Hall,
And he was blanketed by 'Saturday, Beethoven with Solomon's Philharmonic:'
"Here's a recipe for oblivion. Fate may blow me back to my father's old shtetl.
Wind with such resolve, what could go wrong? So nu... my luck... something demonic,"
Cried Teddy, his heart beating so unusually.
"The ice I can no longer see. Such a harsh way to meet with the waitress Gretel, I say,"
Remarked the baker entirely enveloped in the banner.
"We move like dancers Pas de chat... as if I am carried, gingerly, in careful steps.
So nu... I'm a baker in a banner in a Pas de deux... how is it I speak so much ballet?"

VII

In truth, Teddy became a baker in a banner being carried away down Broad,
And exhausted, he appreciated the gesture of a lift down the icy road to the Mills:
"Tell me! Have the Ice Ants returned to show the way to Gretel and Burble Friedel?
Oh, my world... my Olam ... Jody! Pismire! How you carry me; fanfare & frills!"
Said a man snug in aesthetic rug.
"This fellow weighs on my head, Captain! We've much to travel! The pits will itch,"
Said a basso profundo beneath Teddy.

"There remains enough load for you to carry, Captain. There's a head load, a butt load.

For every cobblestone or trolly track this fellow tends to twist, squirm, twitch."

VIII

His came as a grave voice, yet one that belonged to someone strapping, even earthy,

And, though cozy in Beethoven's banner, Teddy fretted about these powerful limbs.

"Allow me to put a rest this baker's restlessness, you Caliban of Columbus.

In a curl I will ease his strain; with a tail tuck, I'll offer a cat nap potion on a whim,"

Offered a higher pitched voice now atop Teddy.

"Your sacrifice seems too great to accept, Captain, for your pounds builds the burden,"

Said the deeper voice.

"Off grey fur ball! Go shed off in the eastbound wind. Westbound fur blanks our path.

Cats snooze nose to buttock, Captain. You'll sleep long to who knows when, perhaps to ten."

IX

Teddy determined that the time arrived to discuss matters with his chatty taxi,

And he cried out from the banner, startling the so-called captain into a leap:

"Put me down, you springy trap! I am a baker on a mission to find the right onion.

Free me from this banner and I will allow to go off into winter without a peep,"

Demanded Teddy, wiggling about like a cat in a bag.

"Mensch, I believe we have been commanded and we should let him see the light,"

Said the Captain to his companion.

"After all, what light we might show will only be a start. It's Burble Friedel he seeks.

Greetings bundled baker! How startled you must be to have golem with cat within sight."

On his feet, Teddy faced an orange, rutted bemouth, accompanied by a grey cat,
And, feeling the brittleness of cold again, decided to hear a proposal for a truce:
"Herr Baker, I am, as you suspect, the Golem that viewed your life via a window.
My captain, Captain Ketzele calls me Mensch, yet Burble Friedel calls me Bruce,"
Said the Golem, scratching at his armpits.
"On behalf of all misnamed Golems, I introduce you to naval war hero, Captain Ketzele,"
Reported Mensch or, should one say, Bruce.
"On the Island of Coocoos, this captain here meowed, warning his mates of a mutiny.
Though I may have some of the better details in a haze... Care for a pretzel?"

Bruce searched his body for the offered pretzel but could find only pebbles,
And, apologizing for his faux hospitality, continued to share Ketzele's war escapades:
"For graceful gallantry, the captain became Captain but not without misfortune.
The pinning of medals has hazards, as Captain soon found his way to the stockade,"
Said the Golem with a respectful grin.
"For when the General pinned Ketzele's breast, Captain nipped a colonel's knuckle,"
Said Bruce, starting to laugh, shedding bits of clay.
"After ten days of sardines, water, and loneliness, haughty brass visited Captain Ketzele.
'So a lesson's learned, mouser?' asked a boss. 'Or are you collecting kitty paw carbuncle?'"

To beat the wind, the trio continued to slip down Broad Street towards the Mills Café,

And Bruce continued to share Captain Ketzele's naval exploits, his feline magnificence:
"Good Captain Ketzele rose into a brilliant stretch – a cat pose to shame any aspiring yogi.
My hero Bogart would have approved the Captain's naughtiness, his feline maleficence."
Reported Bruce to an astonished baker and proud cat.
"Upon a prison bed, Captain Ketzele yawned, correcting their usage of the word 'stockade.'
Laughed Bruce in the telling.
Every fellow at the cinema knows, navies send bad eggs off for a stint in the brig.
This he said chasing, swatting at dangling epaulets all through this obvious prison raid."

XIII

Bruce jumped, swaggered, laughed, flaked, eroded, all while acting the role of a cat,
And, hitting a precise piece of ice, flopped & slid down the next Broad Street block:
"YO HO! Ohio River bound! Call up a paddle wheel Captain. Shall a clay man float?
There's the Mills, just in time for a little lunch, for I believe it's past noon o'clock,"
Said Bruce, pointing to a café with plywood over widows.
"I dream of cottage cheese over a pineapple slice, packaged wafers, downed by tea,"
Said the Golem frothing after a skid.
"Imagine the milk, Captain. Imagine the widest bowl, lapped by the steamiest of windows.
Imagine the milk, baker! The divine potion for all you figure! Wouldn't you agree?"

XIV

The trio stepped into the Café, quickly admiring the massive painting filling a wall,
And, moving between tables, took in the trifecta aroma of stale coffee, oatmeal, sugar:

"Psst! Bruce! Master Baker Cream Horn. Say Nothing! Act normal. Lick your wrists.
Here staggers the waitress Gretel, head aimed where we need travel further,"
Said the Cat to his fellow travelers who then, well, licked their wrists.
"Captain Ketzele, perhaps your usual... an egg scramble, with an indulgence of lox,"
Uttered Gretel, her voice strained by her headiness.
"Bruce, we've saltines in the wrappings you love. Sadly, our pineapple all froze.
For this new friend, hot tea; he shivers like an earthquake casting about rocks."

XV

A tiny woman wearing a bright red uniform traveled with her head forever twisted,
And she carried, in ever so slight steps, a plate of cottage cheese & wafers, for the Golem:
"Fish from a feline perspective seems imperative... the significance of lox impregnable.
Succulent to think of it... wait... I see Spirits... as when in combat mission in Holland,"
Chimed in Captain Ketzele.
"Blessing on the lox... Spirits again... or was it in the fight for the city of Bonn?"
Said the confused, combative cat.
"Gretel, Bruce, Teddy. Devour your crackers! Gulp your tea! Teddy's to find the onion...
Means a ride with Burble Friedel to the Sepulcher's Café. But first I must respectfully yawn."

The Ballad of Captain Ketzele

(As sung by Bruce, accompanied by Ketzele's Fleas, with fleeing harmonica)

Bruce:
'Twas as Ensign Ketzele he did board,
A furball amongst a sailing hoard.
the battleship in Bad Abendessen
Sailed for Atlantic war... a thousand men,
On the Battleship Berliner....

Fleas:
Ich bin Berliner

Bruce:
With sailor's cue was Ketzele welcomed aboard,
That sailors today sing of what was – in atonal chord.
For though 'twas Ensign Ketzele was the very first Ketzele
With singing a 'Twas... seasickness turned her into a feline pretzel,
on the Battleship Berliner....

Fleas:
Ich bin Berliner

Bruce:
With guns all mighty the Berliner did prowl
The Atlantic with discipline & Scowl.
Still parties kept morale quite fitter.
Dancers rubbed feet in Ketzele's cat litter,
On sandy decks of the Berliner

Fleas:
Mao!

Bruce:
Oh, the smell of dancers' feet.

Fleas:
The smell of dancers' feet....

Bruce:
A storm, it was said, blasted the ship.
Men fear drowning like Ahab's Pip
From the sandy deck the captain was swept,
His carcass the ocean forever kept.

Fleas:
OOOOOOO OOOOOO OOOOO

YEHHHHHHHHHHHHHHHHHH

(Mit Harmonica)

"Oh Gott," he cried. "If I could only fly."
Nor could he float, for he did die.
Oh, the Battleship Berliner.

OOOOOO OOOOOO OOOO
He did dieeeeeee…...
AHHHHHHHHHHHHHHHHHHH

Bruce:
Sorn in as Captain without pause,
Ketzele saluted his men.

Fleas:
Did Salute with left paws.

Bruce:
The captain in office then slept,
Upon ramparts wave swept,
Till the battleship Berliner
Ran against a Norway rock.
The battleship, she sunk, taking all that once was.

Fleas:
'Twas no longer the Berliner…

A Solo Basso Flea:
Blahhhhhhhhh!

Book 2
Scene 1
Mishpokhe Mashugga

I

With a steady eye, Bruce balanced piled cottage cheese on the edge of a wafer,
And, despite a twitching nose over lox, Ketzele kept optics on prevailing spirits:
"Heaven is stacking curds on high! I've chipped pearls from the Dover cliffs!
Oh, the crunch of the wafer. Straight from cellophane in a bite I clear it,"
Marveled Bruce, flicking a curd at the mesmerized captain.
"Were these to be onions, Mr. Teddy Baker Man, then I've mounds of pearls,"
Mused the Golem, gathering a straw from a nearby dispenser.
"Lovely word, pearls, certainly Golem royal. Gretel has a way with pearls.
With toast crushed, I declare; let future events, holy and not, roundly unfurl."

II

A tubular paper cannon rose, setting an exact ark for unsuspecting targets,
And the Golem fired cracker crumbs through the straw, at the cat and baker:
"Never waver nor waffle over the promise of wafers… here flies the salt.
Yet, waver when one waffles over a promise… oh, it's many a scratch I hanker,"
Said Bruce scratching his flaking armpit.
"I've dry clay every winter yet to moisten, and matzoh threatens to bind me."
Whined the Golem, after firing one last shot of cracker shrapnel at a dining captain.
"How many salt smidgins filled the sea between myself and proper Golem destiny?
Far too many soupçons upon soupçons upon soupçons for us sensitive beasts to see."

III

Ketzele deftly batted away every crumb shot his way; Teddy took two in the forehead,
And Gretel, oddly amused, threatened to toss the earthen ruffian from the Mills Café:

"By the crook of my neck, I see you, Golem Bruce, a felonious monk at work.
With the weight of this grey braid, Solemn Bruce, I commend your ghastly spray,"
Said Gretel, sauntering to a now wrecked table.
"Oh Gretel, the Little Red House, the Little White House, yellow stars over slain hearts,"
Said a tearing Earth creature.
It was my clay-bound nature to save the weak, wreck shysters until the Rabbi says no more.
This icy day reminds; I missed a Golem's righteous deed, failed a Golem's Beaux Arts."

IV

Gretel listened attentively to Bruce, patted him on his rutted shoulder, took aim,
And flicked a package of pumpernickel bread sticks at the miserable monstrosity:
"Have some nasal brushes, Mensch! Clean out your volcanic mucus streams.
Recall deep oceans, Bruce; it's far better to shine your beloved behemoth gleam,"
Said Gretel sternly yet reassuring.
"Land by the miles before the camps… too many steps for one Golem to trek,"
Continued the grey-eyed waitress.
"No earthy misplaced Golem could paddle or backstroke the Atlantic pond.
Settle with your limitations! Celebrate roses! Celebrate Cheese! Drop the dreck."

V

Bruce fired another round of salt, landing in Captain Ketzele's oldest wound,
And, with a swishing grey tail, the war hero of legend hissed at the offending Golem:
"Gritty Gretel, I wish for an even greater praise shower, lest I blast Ketzele again,"
So I shine! So I look clay fantastic! So I be Mensch! So too I wish my aim a new proem,"
Replied the Golem, searching his plate for a curd or a crumb.
"Yet what is the Mensch, the Bruce, when the Golem's a mere pearl on the edge of toast?"

Continued the terra cotta Cartesian.
"Everybody act normal… pull at your nails with your teeth! Bruce is eroding philosophic,"
Chimed in the caustic cat.
"Rub your head furiously with a moist paw… repeat, ignore the Golem… repeat!
We Cat Collective must then groom a second side… that's my mew, Golem, tautologic."

VI

Ketzele's eyes grew wide as remarkable figures stepping from the colossal mural,
And, bearing brown waistcoats, toques covered spirited gags with checkered cravats:
"Gadzooks! Shag-Bags! I was painted with a wild wedgie in my breeches…
Lucas, good sir, a tug. Years on the wall, I've twisted thingumabobs, a tangled gavotte,"
Moaned one fellow, struggling to regain some sort of form.
"Burnt mutton? A veil of grease I wore while in portrait. My! This inn's aromatic,"
Said one fellow while another stripped down to his shirt, complained.
"My muscles have been rippling for days, for nights. I was framed for my sinew.
We three Haversack boys say without question, hanging in portrait, quite traumatic."

VII

It was clear from the start that only Ketzele viewed the Haversack apparitions,
And, boy, if ever a cat's hair rose, the captain set new records for height:
"Misguided guides, from an old river you rose… but why this season?
It's ice only… fields are now streets. Your sunny dreamscape fails to light,"
Said Ketzele, setting on Orloff's chest, pushing her paws at the baker's chin.
"Awake, Master Cream Horn… do you expect a turtle to carry your world?"
Said the cat, her claws clipping the baker's flesh.
"These are pioneer ghosts, straight from the glory books of your school days.
In their painted fantasies, they sent old forests down river in float & birle."

Teddy's head floated backwards from the tremendous push of the cat's paws,
And Ketzele's blue-grey eyes peered directly into the baker's rounded pupils:
"I see, a baker's blood dribbles much like a cat's, though Golems seldom bleed.
Recall this lesson: honest words need flow otherwise lest nations wallow futile,"
Said the cat to the baker, in Shakespearean chic.
"AH! KETZELE! My jaw, my bagel-tester. How will I know real from the watered?"
Shrieked the baker.
"Such differences determine polite society... Oh! Desquamate... cat's claws shave skin.
These ghosts you see – only a cat sees – registers horrific, otherwise why so bothered?"

IX

Stunned by apparitions appearing in such gaudiness Ketzele dug from flesh to muscle,
And flashing emerald ferocity, her eyes widened, her paws rapidly stamping the baker.
"A cat's purr remains preferred, Mademoiselle Le Chat! Yea, preferred. Dig if you must!
I'll sit, suffer, count headlights whisking past... a good night only for a Studebaker,"
Said the Baker, cringing.
"Should you need leave scars...please leave them shaped like rugelach in a neat row,"
Requested Teddy.
"I see your green spheres alarmed. Say what you see, share what most never really see.
Oh, harsh, the pins on your paws! Here's a change of fate: the baker's the dough."

X

Three colonial spirits, in oiled waistcoats, stood before Ketzele as Gretel raised a broom,

And each shook out tightened limbs strained from posing within a fading painting:
"Ah, Madame Feline forgive the entrance, but we've witnessed salt firing, sans peter.
We appointed pioneers know a thing or two, though our education came with some caning,"
Said the muscled phenomenon.
"Tread carefully the vibrations of polemics, epistemics, pandemics, yet save the endemics,"
Said another rendered spirit.
"Question catatonics, however droll. Cuddle the ironic… hug the symbolic, honor the allegoric.
Revel in tonics. Handle, by George, halleluiah-like histrionics. Relish Biblical acrostics."

XI

So said a third spirit, wearing painted tan as Gretel swept a morning's floor schmutz,
And Ketzele rose, stretched, yawned, washed body & bits, then addressed the spirits:
"On what pedestal do you sit to give an audience advice? Can an image scratch a chin?
How high or how low does your soapbox go? Do we revere or, cat-like, fear it?"
Argued Ketzele, though appearing as a cat speaking to herself.
"Our pedestal is the very painting on which we have been lofted, these many decades,"
Replied a muscular fellow in shirt tails.
"We know what giants speak, from Governor McKinley to Burble Friedel, feeling bloat.
We've witnessed depraved promises, lawyers relieved, gluttons purging in unusual shades."

XII

Gretel swung her broom over her exposed shoulder, conjuring a fantastic wind,
And swooshed three spirits back into the painting from which they came:
"Friedel? Burble Friedel? You've witnessed the baker's friend Friedel?

The baker needs Friedel for the need of the Grand Onion; at least this is his claim,"
Said Ketzele, suddenly hopping off the baker.
"The Golem, yea, a Golem needs the same bulb to pack away genuine guilt in socks,"
Continued the captain of vessels quite decommissioned.
"Which leaves the needs of one perfectly grey feline, ready to guide a quest. A cat's need of such an onion? Why mew how! The joy... no, the comfort of grand lox."

XIII

Ketzele finished what appeared to others as a soliloquy of a more or less bizarre quality,
And rubbing thick ankles, tickled the Golem into howling about the café, upending chairs:
"Ketzele, rally up your baker, goad your Golem away from plates of too many curds.
Cold will be on you, expect to descend... My,you leave the café too many hairs,"
Said an image, now returned to the painting in colonial purge form.
"Friedel, stands by the morning news, holding roses in winter, by an alley called Pearl."
Continued the image, frozen, though in leafy green landscape.
"We see Burble as diner, often; he comes in to partake of café air inflating his bloat.
Beware! He dragged many down from posterity onto posteriors, in quick hurl."

XIV

Ketzele reached to scratch at the painting but was quickly carried away by Bruce,
And Gretel stored away her broom with thoughts trickling ever so towards a boil:
"Be still captured, Captain Ketzele. For what do you wiggle? For whom does your fur fly?
No wind will ever twist metal into such shapes that I see now in your cat coi,"
Said Bruce, suffering the swings and spears of an outraged cat.
"You have nothing to fear but my fur itself! Now are you done,"

Said Ketzele, with a clear and present growl.
"Wired Ketzele! Crusted Bruce! Sleepy Baker! "I heard them, Ketzele, like you!
 So nu! I heard them say a corner of Pearl, perhaps finding Burble in a noon
sun."

XV

Gretel settled the crowd, despite her failing voice, she turning about in the
café,
And shuffling to the back of the restaurant, she pointed at windowed swing
doors:
"So few have ever drifted past these doors, to see what really lives beyond a
Café.
There, you'll find something rich as babka, though marked as these unwashed
floors,"
Said Gretel, about to spill mystery diner beans.
"Sure as Moses stood on Nebo, mesmerized by the view over the sloping
Pisgah,"
Directed the waitress, exchanging her smock for an oversized wool trench
coat.
"Burble Friedel remains a great thaumaturge for an age, even in the grey
Ohio actuality.
His intake of Café air so great, he holds the light; so, we seek him as
Mishpokhe Meshuga."

Book 2
Scene 2
Gretel's Great Neck Lug

I

Pushing through swing doors, the quartet came straight on to sinks, hoses, sponges,
And a disheveled man so grimy he could have been mistaken for a chimney sweep:
"This man scrubs all Café dishes, recites all relevant tales of rightful war, Rich eh?
So nu? Babka Opulent, show tune hummer & our dryer bunny, Bina, working a dish heap,"
Said Gretel, introducing a rabbit at work with a white cotton tail.
"Teddy! Teddy! Teddy Orloff, the last I saw you, my cousin had stormed Normandy Beach,"
Said Richard, his dungarees sagging to expose black-streaked underwear.
"Did you hear of Harvey Boling, choked to death on the powdered sugar...
A Bavarian Cream, I believe... sad ending for eating so fast, a longer life far out of reach."

II

Teddy suggested a Kaddish for Harvey, but they were a few rabbits short of a minyan,
And the baker questioned a dishwasher, once thought bound for Harvard in an Edsel:
"Dear schoolmate, now dishwasher royale, how did you find your latest profession?
What of your war days? What word of our chum, Harvey? So many dishes to jostle!"
Remarked Teddy to the sordid plate scrubber.
"When dishes mount, Bina and I prefer humming Rodgers when he had a nimble heart,"
Said Richard, handing the rabbit a salad bowl to dry.
"My trip to the Café... some strange fellows invite me on a Hoffman bicycle ride,"
Lysergic acid diethylamide... new from Albert's lab... where minds fall apart."

Rich gave an emaciated appearance to the quartet, curious as to what he might say next,
And Ketzele, wrapped up lovingly by the Golem, squirmed in Bruce's gigantic mitts:
"In '43 I was expelled from the Yeshiva for playing Water polo in a mikvah... bad idea.
Too small of a court... broke a fixture or two, sending customarily calm rebbes into fits,"
Said the dishwasher, smirking.
"In '44, Hoffman served a mold on rye, ergot, much too much of which I took,"
Continued Richard, often twitching his head.
"This so common a fungus amongst us gave color, picture to my then bleak world.
But like all things misconstrued as good, love for the mold left me with a permanent shook."

Ketzele twisted her way from the Golem's arms, landing on floor, shaking it all out,
And she ran for the very last door, in sudden need to venture out onto the ice:
"Daily chores became cumbersome... disentangled... simplicity felt like herding golems.
The clicking of clean plates soothes my warped head left only with trivia & eccentricity,"
Said Richard, straight to the baker, though never looking eye to eye.
"What joyous scandals you lived, schoolmate, but what of the companion rabbit?"
Asked Teddy, unable to recall spending any kitchen afternoons with hares.
"I should dry with a kangaroo? This I tried, but marsupial dishwashing have risks.
Surely you realize, a hired Roo's rouse: pocket the plate quick as they could nab it."

Gretel pushed a cart towards Rich, signaling these were the times for bussers to shine,
And Rich silently headed out the swing doors, finding walls spackled with cottage cheese:
"The weight of this café tugs my head closer, closer to the shoulder, Golem, Baker, Cat.
But I've a much greater weight by the day. The camp my left neck limped, my kepi freeze,"
Said Gretel, surprised by her sudden openness.
"Be sure 'scrape, stack, segregate… majestic busser… for this remains café hypothesis,"
Called out Gretel to Rich, he scraping away at curd pellets.
"In exact numbers we were huddled into cattle cars, sixty-five per car, all from Bavaria.
In days, we came to a place called Oświęcim; we need be sixty five, such a number neurosis."

Gretel rubbed her exposed neck, pinching at skin flaps, rubbing exhausted tendons,
And with every caress, her shoulder arched up, flashing fish-like patches of psoriasis:
"Numbers, numbers, numbers, mine I carry in green, forged across my collarbone.
A yellow star, I keep, stitched inside my wired bandeau; think not this as Gretel's Psychosis,"
Said the revered waitress.
"Richard adorns his union suit with earthly blemish – a dirt streak for each million lost,"
Said Gretel.
"Labor, Golem! Labor Ketzele! Labor, baker! All of us in the shadow of an iron signpost.
To carry stones, never, for the sake of lives, to be dropped – in hot sun, even morning frost."

Gretel spoke, shifting in a circle, laying eyes on the Golem... the cat... the baker,
And when making contact with Teddy, waddled up to him, speaking directly to him:
"Then we worked, but to say we were then free... well then that then would be a lie.
Where were you, Golem, when my Selection Day came, Gretel's days already beyond grim?"
Said Gretel, placing a hand on Teddy's shoulder.
"An onion you seek? Burble Friedel you seek? Strip my rags, a command for nakedness,"
Continued Gretel, swinging her head towards Bruce.
"Ah Mensch! You seem such a rock-solid Mensch! What do they seek from my nakedness?
Steel door shut, its creek... three hundred naked... in form as created. Had God forgotten us?"

Bruce cried. Ketzele strolled about Gretel's ankles, Teddy held her hand,
And Bina took to drying the Golem's eyes, leaving a brown smear about his tail:
"In mass, such a frightened collection of mothers, daughters. In mass... crushed together.
Think hot water, Mensch! That we expect from pipes, Ketzele. Gentle drops, baker, not hail,"
Said Gretel, her crowd attentive.
"In mass we wait. We wait more. Then more. We wait as the door creeks once again,"
She said.
"By the neck then! By the neck! A hand reaches inside, takes me by the neck.
Eyes of women watched me dragged further, further out the door, my neck strained."

Gretel reached to hold Bruce's hand, calming the Golem whose remorse grew loud,

And a light flashed through the room allowing the waitress to speak even bolder:
"On the opposite side of the door, I could hear women, children shrieks, unimaginable pitch.
Each scream... my neck bent further, further until my ear forever rested upon a shoulder,"
Said Gretel, tears dribbling off her nose to the floor.
"More water for Richard's plates, eh? Bina, a light on the water, then we find Burble,"
Said Gretel, collecting herself, though her neck hung just as heavy.
"Do Golems cry, Mensch? Will a Ketzele wail? What will a bread maker say of despair?
I speak of my tale loudly – craving to straighten my neck – loud, never non-verbal."

X

Through the swinging doors, Gretel signaled to Richard to fetch his sled,
And Bruce opened the farthest door for Ketzele, whose legs were quite pretzeled:
"As a beauteous sage often said: Don't chase it! Don't kill it! Don't eat it!
Captain Ketzele, beware a slide on the ice while at toilet... return once all is secreted,"
Said the smirking Golem.
"I may be a phenomenal feline, a reputed predator traveling on pads made for stealth,"
Answered the Captain.
"Yet on ice, I confess, I skid like all the rest. God help those nearing the sewers.
I risk a whiz under fragile ice stalactites from dire necessity, not for my health."

XI

Captain Ketzele stood by the open door, extended a nose with thirty twitches,
And, after a Golem's cajoling, she exited to do what all captains must daily do:
"Mensch Golem! Mine! Mine number 199,999... so it says on my wrecked bone.
One number past mine, all started over then over again as the masses grew,"
Said Gretel, peering out the door.

"Here comes Richard's sled. Do you know what it is to carry mud, Mensch Golem?"
Said Gretel, signaling for everyone to climb aboard.
"Here's a special coin, one for each of you, Ketzele, Golem and Baker, one each for a ride.
Richard's sled glides well on such an ice glow; so far better than a gripping mud glum."

XII

The dishwasher's lengthy sled arrived just as Ketzele returned from her respite,
And the quartet stepped upon the boards, each handing over a coin to Richard:
"I say again, Man of Earth… Do you know what it is to carry mud, Mensch Golem?
Do you know, Baker, Ketzele, what it is to carry such sloppy load as if a herd?"
Said Gretel, handing her coin to the driver.
"I have an idea gentle Gretel! As I carry clotted mud from one point to another,"
Replied the Golem, furiously scratching his chin.
"Ha! No beard but crumbs, twigs… Ketzele says 'Twigs do not make beards, clay face!'
But I carry myself as grisly as Fascist Pound. I never shave; too much bother."

XIII

Richard jabbed a giant pole, made with three tightly taped mop handles, into the ice,
And as if gliding on rutted river his sled – a pan dolly on blades – staggered towards Friedel:
"So, the years have found for you a profession, Richard; how you carry-on over the streets.
Whoa! There goes my stomach's bottom… the lox that warms within… a trip hardly dull,"
Said Teddy, feeling his stomach drop as if he were on a rollercoaster.
"You wear filth expertly, Der Steersman Richard. Have you thought of becoming a Golem?
Said Bruce, thinking more such Earth creatures a solid idea.
"I dig at my skin for irritable branches, lodged acorns, sometimes scratching the night away.

Yet, Steersman Richard... think of a Golem's life pluses... pursuance of the light solemn."

XIV

Richard did not answer Bruce's social queries but continued to push the sled further to Friedel,
And Gretel, having been silent for a street or two, spoke in surprisingly exuberant tones:
"Who shall we find with Burble? Kukameyne? Ganif? Mensch? A Pearl in the Alley, Shnoror?
Do you think, Baker, he has the means to reveal the onion, or will his heart be of stones?"
Said Gretel to Teddy, who was struggling to keep on his feet.
"Well, Gretel... therein lies how this will roll out. Burble a Gonif perhaps, never a Shnoror,"
Said Teddy, thinking he saw a hand reaching out from the frozen streets.
"Whimsey, says Burble Friedel, with such knowledge of fantastical onions, lives crafty.
Curing my ailing brood grips my cerebellum; my covering hair matches the ice's hues of hoar."

XV

Richard's sled arrived at the Alley's entrance, clunking straight into gapping pothole,
And, eye-level with the street, the passengers surveyed bricked path for Burble Friedel signs:
"Master Cream Horn! What say you in return to a babbling metaphor driving a sled?
In the Pearl, find a burly fellow droning, 'Anna Mae! Anna Mae...' she for whom he pines."
Said Richard, peeling a gold coin.
"Baker Teddy, onions gleam in the right light. Seek the sewer with wedged three bulbs lit,"
Continued the sled driver, finding chocolate within the coins.
"Gretel, for such delectable coins, I humbly thank you. Ketzele, watch your paws upon exit.
Bruce, Mensch, Golem... allow yourself forgiveness... forever embrace the gelt, chocolate!"

Book 2
Scene 3
Burble Friedel Flies a Bloat

I

Cleared of the sled, the quartet gingerly stepped into the alley, fearing a harsh slip.
And Richard, with some assistance from Bruce, righted his sled and returned to the Café:
"May you find the onion, Baker Teddy. Climb light after light, but perfection... Teddy...
Perfection... that's an endless path... Yet, for the right latke never settle, never sway,"
Called out Richard as he sledded away.
"To say you have found Burble is to say you have found a man carrying thirteen roses,"
Said Gretel, curious as why her head had risen from her shoulder.
"Like Grimm's babies laying crumbs from home through an uncertain forest, Burble Friedel lays one by one rose petals leading to the three onions ripe for noses."

II

With Richard's bony essence completely out of sight, Gretel lead all alley bound,
And, holding to concrete walls, they shuffled towards tones of magnificent drumming:
"All told! Bikini blew! All told! Bikini blew! Beware the *Beast with Five Fingers*, Amalek's near! The beast of beasts! All told! Bikini blew! Amalek's bopping, humming,"
Came a voice from a distant alley corner.
"Follow, stanchly fellows, that troubled voice but look not into Burble Friedel's gut,"
Warned, Gretel, her neck locked back into an overhang of her shoulder.
"He, like a rising Wisconsin gasbag, latches onto the worst, revels in shrieks, political pouts.
Watch for his gastro ballooning... polemics make him bloat as a zeppelin in full glut."

Gretel scratched at her neck, edging closer to the racket echoing off building walls,
And Ketzele leaped on her exposed nape, stretching its length in cat-like down dog:
"Damn the 18th! Carry this nation by the sozzled for the sozzled... Oh so sozzled.
Vodka juice instead of Volstead abuse. Oh protest, you're such an intoxicating grog,"
Came the voice growing ragged by the syllable.
"BALUGA! Check the taxes! Check the taxes! Warren G's Bacon's cooked! BALUGA!
Said a shrieking man, his pitch rising higher than Mozart's magic F.
"Sure enough, Burble's stuck in decades long since passed. Friedel embraces the grudge,"
Said Gretel, scoffing at Friedel's dated gripes.
"Friedel inflates the dialectic; his ancient skirmishes swell into perpetual soliloquy brawls.
Word to feline... word to the Golem... word to the baker... Watch slipping in his sludge."

From the alley corner, Ketzele spotted an enlarged man with eyes bulging from polemics,
And, in desperate need to sharpen a claw or two, she ripped at the floating blimp's knee:
"Baaaaaluuuuuuga... oh such weight has drifted from my deflating, particular patellar.
Baaaaaluuuuuuga... my thanks, kind cat, Now a poke at the shoulder; set my burdens free,"
Said the fellow, now shrinking back to the alley's bricks.
"BALUGA! Tell me, teeny cat, tell me true; did you steal airman Lindberg's little pisher?
Said the man, bloating such that he bobbed against fifth floor ceramic adornments.
"The press has lost its mind; camera bulbs flash, flash, flash at courthouse steps.
BALUGA! Your bristled whiskers suggest you are a Bruno – a celebrity's child pincher."

All looked skyward, finding Ketzele licking her paw while upon a dirigible's knee.,
And, with widening eyes, ears pointing backwards, the captain moved slowly upwards:
"I'm neither a Bruno nor a Clyde... hardly a baby face or a bonnie face. I'm a Ketzele!
In fact, I am Captain Ketzele, you intemperate weather balloon, you overblown gourd,"
Said the cat, extending a full five claws.
"What clamoring do you plot up there, cat now afloat with such a demonstrative inflatable,"
Said Gretel, her head comfortably at rest upon her shoulder.
"Do you kibitz with the very Burble Friedel? All I see is the seat of a flying buttress.
Be aware of his musings... street kibitz declares all he says to be kakameyne, quite debatable."

Ketzele grew oddly comfortable to her expanding zeppelin ride, its mouth widening,
And red-faced faced, blasting out a BALUGA and another aged conspiracy conjecture:
"Scope out Tennessee, prickly Mao! Scope, then you'll find nonsense monkeying nonsense.
Thanks for a stab at the patellar, Queen Cat, I am tending to birth a Burble Friedel lecture."
Said the man reveled as the fabled Friedel.
"A good knee – an underpinning to legitimate shouts, purposeful rants, haughty histrionics,"
Said Friedel, believing the cat had managed to relax him thoroughly.
"Baaaaaluuuuuuga... what spell have you placed on me, you miniature fur ball sorceress?
"Baaaaaluuuuuuga... you ease me from polemics to where bliss with glee commix."

Losing his hot air, Burble Friedel settled upon bricks as another rambler like the quartet,
And Ketzele, finding it time to escape her ride, took to **bunting the baker's ankles:**
"Now an 'Altekaker Trot' by Friedel: wizened words in frolic waltz, such a giddy gambol...
No, for the young from an old man's tongue, here's my Cavort conceived to rankle,"
Blurted Burble, assuming a twisted ballet's fifth position.
"Alley-wise, Friedel, the young have many days ahead to ignore your prancing advice,"
Said Teddy, speaking for the first time in quite a while.
"I've watched you bloat, carry on in a float over ancient worries now quite remote.
As I've hair like my grandfather when a grandfather, it's a special onion that will entice."

Avoiding Ketzele's tail, Friedel searched the baker's head for hair but found none,
And, surveying a bumpy kepi, he certified Teddy's dome carried parental sincerity:
"Such a rutted head deserves applause, for you've five bumps for five fears.
Growing qualms appear as bother bumps... certainly, sir, your deep loving such a rarity,"
Surmised Burble, knocking Teddy's head... giving rise to a sixth bump.
"Ahh! Meshuga... You bopped me... take a powder with your wiseacre gobbledygook,"
Shrieked Teddy, staggering into Bruce's arms.
"I'm just a baker in search of an onion; I'm hardly skating hoping for the concussive.
Hold me, Golem, my knees turn weak, my eyes spin... your head resembles a rocky rook."

Bruce held the baker steady, feeling somehow important to the scheme of things,

And Friedel circled the pair, mumbling meditatively 'if then artichokes have hearts…':

"Onions, what noble bulbs in tunics and scales. Baker, they're such fleshy fellows.

Beneath, Baker, just beneath the tunic, flowering buds wrapped in leafy scale parts,"

Mused Friedel, wiping his brow from peeling back tough layers.

"Pardon the bop upon your head, Herr Baker. A sixth bulging bump beats five fears,"

Said Friedel, embracing Teddy, who was embraced by Bruce.

"A baker, eh? A bikini blow-up baker? Underwater baker bikini blow-up baker, eh?

Meh! Bombs blown underwater amongst the fish, baker, you say? Come near!

X

Try as he may, staggering feet, Teddy could not find a way to be closer to Burble Friedel,

And, as she often chose, Ketzele selected this delicate moment to settle on the Golem:

"I fail to understand your explosive words, Burble Friedel. Encased by ice, I hear but drivel.

I seek the onion to cure the fever infecting my five beautiful little ones. I search solemn,"

Said Teddy, feeling Bruce's embrace was not quite as effective as a thick blanket.

"I wish to soar as I am, Burble Friedel. Yet precise soaring, alas, no one seems to grasp,"

Said Friedel, still embracing Teddy, embraced by Bruce, upon whose shoulder Ketzele sat.

"You should see a doctor for that bump… new bumps allow older such blemishes to fade.

That bump just might leave a life-long mark, very much like Cleopatra's nipping asp."

XI

Teddy rubbed the rising bruise, sensing it a paled pain, hardly rivaling his fears,

And Burble Friedel released the hug, believing he had another argument mounting:
"Icy days are best spent in cuddles... Gretel, Ketzele, step in with this gravelly Golem.
By your ear folds, Ketzele, I spy feline skepticism... a scoffing feral cat pouting,"
Said Friedel, a persuasive gust filling his belly.
"Alley dwelling Friedel, the great battles of a world at war, so many I had seen,"
Interjected Captain Ketzele.
"As officer, I witnessed the Great Christmas Bulge of '44, a beach raid on Iwo! Take it from a veteran feline, I've seen battle horrors, though passed on Kasserine."

XII

Ketzele stood behind Teddy's legs, addressing Burble attempting to bloat once again,
And she piqued about addressing, in staccato chirps, Friedel, who replied in gurgles.
"Call me Mouser Misanthropist, Friedel, Malcontent Moggy to my Pacific battle mates.
Oh, I've read, scratched, wizened about yellowed papers. I know it's our trust you burgle."
Said Ketzele with wind picking away and raising fur.
"Glory, cat, at my silk-encased ankles. Could you be the cure?... my heart suddenly settles,"
Said the baker, feeling joy for the first time on an icy day.
"Captain Ketzele, every brush against me says here's a fur-encased antidote to sadness.
Yours, a heavy burden for such a slight creature, eh, gray one? What say you, Gretel?"

XIII

Gretel turned a shoulder directly at Friedel, addressing him in impatient waitress fashion,
And, in turn, a stunned Burble Friedel gave the petite dynamo his complete attention:
"Where is your rose, Burble? Where is that welcoming light within those sacred petals?

Find the rose, settle the petals – towards the baker's onion – in divine succession,"
Said Gretel, her eyes making direct contact with Friedel's heart.
"Direct your wind, Burble Friedel… free it towards that miracle bulb in elysian field,"
Continued the diner hostess.
"We'll follow together, Golem, Cat, Baker, myself, celestial waitress, in tight procession.
This Alley may be your folly, Friedel. But this onion… it's our quest without yield."

XIV

Cracking knuckles, Burble stretched his taunt facial muscles into his first smile of the day,
And he motioned everyone to leave the Alley, an order countered with the quartet's stares:
"From the Certs Soda Fountain forward, I will place one rose petal followed by another,"
I've thirteen petals to choose… thirteen more than the dotting strands of Mr. Baker's hairs,"
Said Burble with a pinched chuckle.
"Mr. Baker, you speak of the finest onion, a bulb with gracious leaves, a layered remedy,"
Boasted Burble.
"I know of three such bulbs, lined in a row – all guarding the entrance to Amalek's hall.
Watch for the gathering of Wake Snakes; they clash in rhythm when singing a stale elegy."

XV

From a distance, everyone could hear a sled skidding across ice, clipping streetcar rails,
And, from an even greater distance, Ketzele alone heard Richard shouting, 'WAHOO!':
"Gather… we'll saunter over to where brave ants nightly go to munch post-march.
Some advice when near Amalek, keep spare harsh words or else it will be a night to rue,"
Warned Burble, inflating in silent volatility.

"Why need an antidote to self-indulgence when it's an anecdote is all that is needed?"
Advised Burble to his sparse crowd.
"Capture with anticipatory drums every moan, groan & rattle this creature mutters.
Tap then tune your drums to Amalek; humor his excess, then your wishes will be heeded."

The Ballad (Battle) of Gretel's Genuine Menu

Good evening for a hot dinner... it's a good evening besides the cold, I agree... December is a howling month... Would like something other than water... water was never allowed in my earlier days... Selzer?

Oh yes... cake we have... cream cheese makes the frosting... like late October makes a firmer frost affecting the beets and a blessing on the turnips... a proper chill and the cake shall be perfect... drop your spoon... don't bother we find a clean one....

That comes with a soup or an iceberg lettuce salad with saltines... our beets are freshly boiled... In the camps we fought over turnips. In the camps ... Challah we got. For you sir... I am so sorry that we are out of cottage cheese. Selzer?

Oh, I heard all about Rosa... the redhaired as she is... I told her what I thought and now after thirty years, including the Camps, we no longer speak to each other. Still, I say keep the Evil Eye away from Rosa. I'd spit but that would be inappropriate in a café for sophisticated diners like you... Selzer?

Richard... Oh Richard's out back keeping the mice at bay. He's swatting mice burrowing in through the alley... Those long days when we as mice were rendered as stew... as I was saying, cream cheese makes the frosting... roasting like the morning we were sent into Vienna's cobblestone street... cobblestone much like the good Pesach marble cake we have, though Pesach seemed alien when in the camps ...

Ah the Borscht! Cup or a bowl? You can have it as side or have a bowlful. As I said, we boiled our beets... lest we leave them in a pan to burn... How's the pot roast? Excellent, what else? The butcher guarantees never a slice will be treif...

How did I come to America? Certainly you know. All who come to this café came the same way, A breeze here, a breeze there. The winds kept my spirit up as we traveled. Rumor floats we'll be remembered here. I shall put in your memorable choices... Do you wish for something other to drink? Selzer?

I

Then there was more ice. The Quartet, with Friedel, huddled together for a walk,
And Burble assured the quartet that hot jazz could be found in the coldest of places:
"Wait until you hear the band... its honks, its crashes, its boogie-woogie, man.
The band's got the spice. We'll catch a ride with spirits, but beware the zozzled spaced,"
Said Burble, growing a little flush.
"BALUGA! Watch the zozzled, be leery... though sometimes funny like Ray Bolger..."
Continued the man, experiencing inflation...
"You need suspect the zozzled, I say, for this is where the old bottles flow.
BALUGA! Beware the zozzled when wound, when rolling about glassy dead soldiers."

II

The streets remained quiet save a Morning Dove's soft coo bouncing off alley walls,
And Ketzele, startled by the idea of dead soldiers, confided with a protector –
Bruce.
"Clay fills about my anterior naris, a Golem's daily struggle, yet I sense your cat fear.
Someday I must change this nose... but hear the turtle dove, Ketzele; it sings hope, I deduce,"
Said the Golem, soothing Ketzele's qualms.
"Turtle dove... foul flying terrapin... do you wish to build the Ketzele's naiveté,"
Muttered Burble, lifting off the pavement.
"I once rose from bed happy, hearing your song; now I float bloated by every hullabaloo,"
Now I boil quicker than any kettle from the lightest utter, mumble or say..."

Friedel froze on his thesis, threw out his arms, halting the advancing onion-seeking troupe,
And, with a constant squeak, he released contemptuous gas like a dazzled pierced balloon:
"What wide-winged Grif do we have before us, a buzzard too early for Spring now frozen.
Are you here shagging snowballs, thinking a November would mean Spring that soon?"
Said Friedel to a large bird, frozen in his tracks, wings fully expanded.
From here, I planned to swoop into Hinkley, calling all brother Buzzards into a spectacular wake.
Said Grif, thoroughly discouraged by his unnatural plan.
"I thought... arrive just a little early, then Spring would step right up and settle winter away.
Meh, December, I pushed hope towards March 15; now I sit frozen like an ice cream cake."

Burble's nethermost belly zone inflated with a serious, untimely, yes, grotesque guffaw,
And yet, to his surprise, he gathered a righteous gumption to suppress all snorts & sniggers:
"Old friend, Grif! What is this? ... red flares from your wings weighed with icicles anchors?
A blast of blood flowing from humerus, from a broken left... who pulled the gun trigger?"
Asked Burble, horrified by Grif's grim condition.
"I plotted an early flight to Hinkley, paying the freight by selling the choicest vegetables,"
Said Grif, showing what seemed to be mushrooms dangling from his wounded wing.
"Miss Gretel, might I interest you in the delights of distinctive, no, matchless fungi?
From a buzzard's outlet, Miss Gretel, gentle Golem, solemn cat: My shiitake collectables."

V

Extending a buzzard's breast, Grif's opening wings holding things in assortment,
And Teddy, wishing a step towards the onion, studied the display with a wrinkled brow:
"Normally, my wife desires broccoli stems, a fibrous chew I essentially disdain.
This day she requests, Sir Bird, the perfect onion for our five, in a fever when we said ciao."
Reported the baker to the Buzzard.
"Herr Grif, anyone can conclude, with break-neck speed, you've a fungi fraud up to your neck,"
Said Gretel, stepping in front of Teddy.
"Neither my kitchen nor Richard's plates would welcome these fossils, as a side or in sauté.
It's the Grand Onion that's the albatross for our necks. I imagine you know where to trek."

VI

The Buzzard smiled, stepping gingerly towards Gretel, snapping seven stalactite icicles,
And sensing freedom, shook massive wings free of blood, expelling rancid buzzard breath:
"Now for me, your apt attention frees me; I need space to roost then finish this bleed.
From here, I suggest you forge straight across on the ice; mark a way to a lower depth,"
Said Grif, a little blood now dribbling from the reopened wound.
"A cantankerous bullet took me down as I was soaring Hinkley-bound for a lake side cliff,"
Continued the buzzard, despite a throbbing wing.
"Shot over High Street, I was, blasted from the sky while in pursuit of a summer roost.
The Hinkley Hunt came to these city streets, leaving me wounded, frozen in a jiff."

Grif steadied a wing upon the baker, the second wing receiving gentle Golem support,
And the Buzzard pointed towards Richmond's Department Store with pointed beak:
There, the well towards a watery purgatory, see the portal with three bulbs gleaming?
Approach each orb with deference, its layers will guide towards the onion you seek,"
Said Grif, finding his balance.
"Chew the bulb least understood, mouth closed. Swish about its layers; eat for opacity,"
Advised the feathered sage, hawkish with his words.
"Devour voraciously the companion bulbs – one for incorruptibility, the second for depravity.
Chew their layers wistfully… shatter ice from this mailbox… trust 'ity' nouns, trust veracity."

The Buzzard successfully confused everyone, from Gretel to the Golem to the baker to the cat,
And Grif began to flap wings, to take flight for the first time since the shooting incident:
"Fear not a descent into profundity, if you dare… there will be onions if you carry audacity.
Oh bye-the-bye, allow my recommendations as I rise while you go down by coincident,"
Said Grif, elevating easily and thus causing Burble to blush.
"Tonight, hear Seymour Rumps with his Sewer Rats. Amazing band. Bigger than Sinatra,"
Called out the bird, more than fifty feet from the ground.
"Hinkley calls; I must go… but once you're in subterranean, have the carrion mammal special.
Delicious if served not so swiftly, say dead twenty-four hours or more… there's my mantra."

Now more than fifty feet above the quartet, Grif thrilled at the prospect of reaching Hinckley,
And, despite a high-pitched voice, he was able to call out a few more thoughts to those below:
"Gretel, consider a gutsier menu: entrees of fetid flesh, Café sides of slivered moldy muscle.
Oh. the spoils to be had… rotten ribeye for each table or a great deal of prime carrion to go,"
Recommend the soaring raptor.
"Carry in? We do not have carry in. Telephone the Café. Richard will box you carryout,"
Said Gretel, with a professional snark.
"Herr Teddy Baker. To the lower depths, for the onion, we layered four shall descend.
"We've cabbage night, we've turnips too. So, add the Café's call for the grandest onion.
Then, for your feverous five, we'll fry latke so golden you'll carry a merited baker's clout."

All four readied were stopped in their tracks by Grif's blood dripping from above,
And splashing on the Golem's nose, Gretel's neck, Ketzele's tail, the baker's shirt:
"Why, I ask, hemorrhaging, shoot a buzzard when you can jitter bug to delicious jazz?
I am aware that under all the concrete and ice remains hardened bed of Ohio dirt,"
Said the Buzzard, tapping feathers over his wound.
"But time for snoozing in dirt can wait when there's a plate of decomposed mice,"
Continued Grif, finding his first drool since being shot.
"Oh, the Mausolea Club's hors d'oeuvres, delightful food in a such a homey underworld.
Follow white snakes slithering straight into all the darkness a storm sewer might entice."

Grif grew ready to soar over the street, grab a breeze for a jaunt to the great lake,
And Burble, holding a rose skyward, wished to join the bird, hoping to argue in Hinkley:
"There go the snakes, straight into the well; shed your petals Friedel, shed them free.
Mark the path to a glowing oblivion, I mean to the Baker's Grand Onion... I flee!"
Called Grif, disappearing into a bleak horizon.
"Wait, Buzzard buddy! You carry on too far. Wait for the Burble to rise like donut dough,"
Shouted Friedel, recklessly dropping rose petals to the opening of the storm sewer.
"Quick, Baker... say something to boil my blood, churn me to be mad as a hornet...
"To fly off the tallest handle. Send me steaming through a roof; let's have a verbal row."

Friedel prepared to inflate with pointless rage as Teddy considered aimless controversy,
And Ketzele conferred with Bruce, who conferred with Gretel, who instigated a melee:
"Burble! As grisly concentration bent my neck, you're the standard barrier of witlessness.
Buzzards carry a better intellectual menu! Yours, the think buffet from a Gimcrack Café,"
Uttered Gretel's insults to Friedel ears.
"BALUGA! Gretel! BALUGA! You insulted the right censors; Oh, sweet jabs, the slyest of sins,"
Said Friedel, inflating and rising towards Grif in a buzzard's holding pattern.
"For such an honorable slight, I humbly advise your path to the Grand Onion, Mr. Baker.
Enter the famed Nut House. Go past the three bulbs, see Amalek himself beating on the skins."

Friedel rose, thumping the Golem's nose as Grif caught the alley sage with spiked talons,
And, flapping with extra weight, rained petrified mushrooms and blood over the petals:
"Grif, I've always admired your yellow trousers... you'll appear fancy at the Hinkley wake.
Oh, I've never noticed your lovely brown eyes; beauty as you devour the dead, it unsettles,"
Said Burble, round as a globe.
"I've a secret held within, Gretel. Your cook uses too much salt. It makes for brackish rats,"
Added the rising Burble.
"There's salting a fish and then there's salting a fish. It need not last until the bomb arrives.
Honor your lovely wife, Mr. Baker.Broccoli stems are delicious... farewell little cat...."

The pair floated off towards the wrong river and, most likely, off to the Minnesota Hinkley,
And remaining quartet turned their sights to a sewer neighboring Richmond's awning:
"Our petals are now speckled petals, a decorous path to a wild world. Shall we go?
Gretel never nods, yet grins. The Golem adjusts his nose, and Ketzele says yes by yawning,"
Said the baker, taking the lead.
'Let's swallow excess fear, send straight into the gut... then walk like upon Burble's petals,"
Advised Teddy on point, Gretel second, Bruce third, and Ketzele wrapped about his neck.
"Tainted... we walk a tainted line... Grif's fungi gore makes a different trail to the well.
Under a mushroomed rose sits a rose... snub bloody buzzard spots... ingest that as mettle."

Unclear as to what Teddy meant, the quartet edged petal by petal to the sewer's edge,

And tucked, as hoped, they spotted three onions glistening in the day's first sunlight:

"Herr Baker at your feet… there goes the afternoon's white snakes into an unknown cellar.

Scamps! Rascals… It's Trouble! It's Hurt! It's Malice, slithering in as our guides outright,"

Said Gretel, stepping sideways, allowing the serpents to pass.

"Snakes or scaley spaghetti this, where we need enter. Ho! **Your paws are cold, Ketzele,**"

Said the Golem, the cat kneading at clay shoulders.

"Mr. Baker, a Rebbe once whispered skins of the Onion are solid like wrapping cloth…

…to preserve the core… The core then is the light you seek. Let's descend for the thrill."

Book 3
Scene 2
Nibbled to the Core

I

Dazzled by light refracting off three bulbs, Ketzele felt compelled to chase a beam,
And, leaping from the Golem's shoulder, kicked clay chips straight into Gretel's smock:
"Burden me not with your excess, Herr Golem. 'Taint not what's saved for drips from my brow.
I've dinners to cook tonight, so dirty me up again and I'll give your clay chin a knock-knock,"
Said Gretel, speaking in fear of the dark sewer ahead.
"You're mine fair brilliance... no, you're mine... 'til I'm bored; I'll snatch your ray onion glow!"
Meowed Ketzele, pouncing as beams changed with drifting clouds.
"What? Bird call.. Ah! Itch beyond the ear... EH? Floating before me a visage of salty lox.
Slab of lox, I see... divine deli Pisces! Feline fantasy! Lox! Lox! Lox! My tongue's in tow."

II

Drooling, Ketzele stepped close to the middle onion, sniffed, raised a paw, gingerly swatted,
And, snapping out needle-like claws, she went to work ripping away at onion layers:
"Lox nest demon... he dwells in every deli, tormenting calicos to torties to tabbies.
Within every onion there must be a ruby fish... so says any worthwhile sooth-sayer,"
Said Ketzele, ripping away at the middle onion.
"What's this I see? Old Scioto banks... coal barges waking waves... lapping at my head,"
Whispered the Golem, eyeing the onion on the left.
"Here, Rebbe Zwi molded me from lumps of Scioto clay, where I lazily passed on every sight.
I, nom de plume Bruce, face what drags and seek a different dress, for sleep in a bloomed bed."

The Golem then laid his earthen girth upon the ice, rolling to the sewer's narrow opening,
And facing the left onion, he fancied plucking a water lily, placing it behind an ear:
"Inhale all that is cold, I shall... Oh, it's folly for Golems to know tranquil air from roused.
They live without taste... say friends, this sewer's mouth seems too narrow to enter here,"
Moaned Bruce, gazing closer and closer to the radiant bulb.
"Catnip glory, such layers must be nepeta cataria. WORT! WORT! WORT! Purely Mint!
Moaned Ketzele, rolling her head upon shreds of onion skin.
"Oh, Gretel and Baker! Come roll your heads. Such is the road to a real stone, Golem Bruce.
I've the sudden need to knead... I knead for need... oh Baker, Gretel, why such eyes asquint?"

Ketzele frantically ripped, rolled then ripped again at the onion, exposing its core,
And Teddy surveyed the sewer's opening, avoiding eyeing the third gleaming bulb:
"Gretel, certainly these spheres have a different purpose than making medicinal latkes.
Say! Why should strains of the 'Emperor Concerto' worm about my head? Brain exults,"
Said the baker, ear far too close to the onion on the right.
"Oh, Herr Baker, I hear its Rondo! And Rondo! And Rondo! How it blankets in flow,"
Reveled Gretel with a longing for a world now destroyed.
Richard shall craft up a feast in its honor, Allegro Eggs, with Rondo Hash, diner delicacy.
Perhaps Ludwig Lox Salad... Yet, new menus aside, do I see the Middle Onion grow?"

Gretel then the baker witnessed – as Ketzele scratched the bulb – its core expanding,
And the larger the sallow bulb grew, the greater the opening to the storm sewer grew:
"Such are the reasons felines scratch, claw, tear... to open doors to a great escapade.
Now we have an avenue wide enough for even graceless Golems to scramble through,"
Said the baker, relieved to have finally found the truth behind cat deconstruction.
"The Queen, she's got some lovely wings! YOU'RE RIGHT! So, drones howl & sing..."
Came a chant near Teddy on his knees, peaking in the sewer, seeing only darkness.
"...YOU'RE RIGHT! Troops! Mandibles on the cards then, with bluff, up the ante.
Mr. Baker, man upon his knees... tort or torte? Pray, which, now life's on the downswing?"

Jody's cadence filled Teddy's ears as the baker crawled over to greet the colony leader,
And, spotting the onions, Jody commanded the column to begin a day's collection:
"Icy days make for slim picnics, Mr. Baker. So, we thought to seek Amalek's hospitality.
These bulbs we'll nibble our way to the core, end the day with a purely sweet confection,"
Said Jody as the ants gorged onions, right and left.
"Munch to the core, careful. Should you need to drop ant tears, please tear gracefully aside,"
Ordered the lead ant.
"Ant inclination clues me to me consider, the core is the way to Amalek's jamming band.
So, rip, chew, tear, save room for dessert. Soon, we'll escape the ice, find warmth inside."

The onions quickly shrunk as skins, shredded layers were carried away by crying ants,
And the colony sobbed... even the mighty Jody wailed... their tears freezing into ant igloos:
"Now Mr. Baker, we have left you shimmering cores that seem to be growing by the second.
It's best to enter now, before the cores diminish. Enter, be dazzled, relish fantastical view,"
Said Jody, signaling for the ants to raise their spoils and march into strangeness.
"Watch for the reptiles, watch for flailing cobwebs, step skeptically about the madness,"
Said Jody, his voice trailing off as the ants vanished.
"Enjoy a hearty nosh. Touch but save the herring for any displaced, digging colliers,
And should you find sappers, making ladders, recognize them for their discreet noblesse."

As any ant might portend moments ahead, Jody proved to be the colony's clairvoyant,
And, interlocking legs, the colony lowered a few hundred, as a ladder to the catacombs:
"Seer, Sir Jody, I am most impressed... do you carry about you a reference oracle to boot?
Or do you walk about icy landscapes, a natural diviner? Or do I speak dialogue in gnome?"
Asked Teddy, thrilled by how the ants engineered.
"We anticipated spoils magnifico, Mr. Baker! Imagine slices of boiled cake, vintage 1932,"
Replied the head ant, waiting his turn on the ladder.
"The trick to descending on such a ladder is to never step on too many of the family's heads.
Should you step on one, promise them early dibs on all table crumbs tossed into floor view."

His turn at the ladder came at last; he had waited for several thousand colleagues to pass,
And Jody – fantasizing solid creamed chipped beef – on the first ant's head:
"Oof there, Jody, put on a nanogram or two... indulge in too much of that old, boiled cake?
Watch the fellows as you step... easy man, these are the chaps you have courageously led,"
Said the first ant holding the ladder.
"Well, Ketzele, certainly one would never find a ladder of golems let alone ladder of cats,"
Said Bruce to the cat, to which she replied, 'Mew.'
"Then a ladder of bakers might lean sensical for those Jacobs climbing could rise in the least.
A Gretel ladder would lean, constantly creak, I suspect, but each step, delightful. Hey, hi-hats."

Not only could they hear hi-hats, toms, cymbals thundering in the darkness, but snares too,
And the quartet began their own descent into the sewer, without the aid of the ant ladder:
"Chrome Dome, rev up your appetite. I've word there may have a barrel or two of Hoover Stew.
Yes, it may appear to your palette a little old, solid... but its quality is in all the latest chatter,"
Said an ant to Teddy, while hustling to join his mates.
"Where in America can you find such rancid delicacies? Here, by golly, in this here swell sewer,"
Continued the ant, now far behind the larger beings.
"Look about you, Teddy Baker Man. In the last sewer flood, loads of armored heifers, unused.
Ignore any brown finless trout passing by; there's much about to collect and serve on skewer."

Gretel reached the sewer's floor first, followed by Teddy, then Bruce with Ketzele in tow,

And looking up to where a little light still emanated, they witnessed a millipede grab up Jody:
"Oh horrors! Arthropod assault! Millipede mugging! Begone, you redundant leaf eater!
Tip-toe elsewhere, you segmented pill! Now's hardly a time for your needs, randy toady,"
Called out Jody as the millipede curled, attempting a half-nelson on the ant.
"Oh, Jody, but you promised a wrestle, should you ever appear in Amalek's lair again,"
Replied the millipede to the trapped ant.
"And here you are, dear, nearly pinned on an ant ladder, trapped by superb arm control.
So, cutie bug, ready for my arthropod-like clamping supremo? It's this match I feel you yen."

XII

Jody squirmed himself free, pushed off legs, several of which poked him in sensitive spots,
And, standing on the millipede's back, walked the tremendous length of passionate creature:
"Carla! Carla! How about two old tins of army strawberries, straight from the war itself?
Stealing away with me... days of wrestling... well, it transcends standard procedure,"
Pleaded Jody to his multi-layered suitor.
"I am committed to my troops... my... my colony... oh don't look at me with sleepy eyes,"
Begged Jody, his heart melting quickly.
"Oh, damn it all, Carla. Come with me... we'll seek maple leaves in aged Hoover Stew.
Then we'll wrestle--a millipede/ant extravaganza... But please. Carla, just remember my size."

XIII

Two tins slapped faces as Carla twisted away from Jody, her body suddenly lifted up high,
And the bighearted millipede was wafted away by the colony's anonymous minions:

"Wrestling on the ant ladder has long been our tradition, ever since this ice age began.
It's a flawed theological metaphor, for sure, but I learned kindness at ant cotillion,"
Said Jody, ready to move on.
"So, waiting friends know they toss free peanuts all about the Nut House... such a bounty,"
Said the ant, now a good distance away.
"Yet, watch for obscurity, revel in ambiguity, cringe at all that's off pitch. This hall's wild.
Baker, Waitress, Golem, Cat; too much rhythm often shakes an ant into another county."

XIV

Teddy turned to his companions, making certain they wished to continue down the sewer,
And each, in their own way, said something about curiosity, which concerned Ketzele gravely:
"In the afternoon of a morning, when my children wake ill, an onion ordered for the cure...
A day in which I've been rolled in posters, ridden an ice ferry, conversed with ants, plainly,"
Said Teddy, graciously.
"I've torn away many thoughts about who travels these plots, see within what they carry,"
Continued the baker with a smile.
"We've been belabored by blowhards, briefed by buzzards, amused by a millipede named Carla.
This city sheds us to the core. The Onion is nigh. It's the old fears we must together bury."

XV

Cobwebs, swayed by a breeze, stroked Ketzele's whiskers, causing the grey cat to sneeze,
And, contorting into odd forms, she choked out upon Bruce's shoulder, a cylinder hairball:
"Share, fellows, share any floating plans as to how to collect the Onion without incident.

You see, fellows, now's the time for sharing; after all, it's Amalek we'll meet down this hall,"
Said Gretel, appearing slighter than usual.
"Cover your scrapes, hide any insidious wounds. Amalek has severe bite, a special craving,"
Said Gretel, looking eye to eye to eye.
"He haunts cooks grating potatoes, seeking, upon inspection, deliciously scraped knuckles.
Oh, Onion seekers, Amalek, Keeper of the Bulb, a blood licker where torn skin's waving."

I

Thundering noise greeted the quartet as they entered the sewer's muddy depths,
And Ketzele's silver eyes, surveying tunnels, found no sight of snakes or Jody's ants:
"My ears bend to my southernly; I hear the voices say, 'Welcome to the Nut House.'
My! Step lightly, for before us, three sloshed slugs, how they booze, rumble out rants,"
Said the cat, considering a slimy snack.
"One minute we're munching on grassroots, the next we're drowning in dishes of beer,"
Cried the slugs in unison.
"Then dumped within porcelain walls, we're awash in a whirlpool, chaos by a chain tug.
We're the Lush Brothers, we love to sing! Do hold off any inklings of a Bronx Cheer."

II

Finding a compromised pitch, the trio set to sing their theme song, in sluggish harmony,
And tuning to the twang of a soggy leaf, they let loose a drinking song in pilfered tune:

> "Three sloshed slugs! Three Sloshed slugs!
> See how they booze! See how they booze!
> They all fell into the brewer's cup
> He bopped them all with a mighty bop
> Three sloshed slugs! Three sloshed slugs!"

"Many apologies for our disturbing slug song; it's our world. Please, please don't impugn."

Tinny horns, along with bleak drumming, filled the well, knocking several bricks loose,
And the slugs were the only sentient creatures able to maintain any sense of balance:
"Fellows, racket aside, lend me your ears... I have traveled seeking a certain vegetable.
I'm a shy baker with children reddened by fever; I seek an Onion, a most superior shallot,"
Said Teddy to the slimy trio.
"Ah! I've no ears to lend. I lent them once to a cute bug, never to have them returned,"
Quipped the Slug.
"Off to the noise. Mind the ruddy floors; don't trip... yet, see the light, oh so fantastic.
Above, you'll find feet dangling from those cursed long ago – frozen instead of burned."

With Bruce on point, the quartet slowly stepped off to the noise, hearts filled with reticence,
And, Bruce, to break the tension, started to tickle the bare feet jetting from the ceiling:
"Little toes, the end of hefty sinners, I suppose. A tickle for wrath, a tickle for sloth.
A tickle for gluttony, a tickle for lust. It's a Golem's amusement, such fun, so appealing,"
Said the Golem as shrieks filled the tunnel.
"Come, Golem, leave the poor souls to dangle. We've an Onion to find in this dank,"
Said Gretel, as Ketzele wrapped around Bruce's shoulders.
Herr Baker, your patience has kept me curious as to how this lively day will resolve.
We peel as we go: Ketzele's hair, the Golem's girth. What do you loose from your tank?"

V

Teddy thought carefully before answering the café entrepreneur's probing question,
And, coming to a fork in the tunnel, he deferred to Gretel as to how to make a difference:
"There are streams of pulsing clatter from either path, both shaking as much as the other.
To find the Onion, I say let us go down this hall, though this nice one deserves deference,"
Said Teddy to his assemblage.
"Four wanderers... one of earth, one of fur, two of uneven flesh... stop in your tracks, I say!"
Came a coarse voice.
"The Onion you seek thrives within layers, rattles with beats, justly flavors Amalek's fillers.
This hall leads merely to more halls, bricks, endless bricks. So respectfully, go the other way."

VI

They chose a hall shaking, rattling, rolling more than others, certain this made a difference,
And the Golem tickled more feet as they moved closer to inviting timpani, snares, kettles:
"More little toes to vellicate: a tickle for envy, a tickle for pride. A tickle for all that's greed.
Ketzele, swaying your tail doubtfully, you say, 'who says vellicate, in our humble Ohio shtetl?'"
Said Bruce with a slight laugh, dislodging more earth.
"Even a Golem finds comfort in tall stacks; my words grow from a nearby book museum,"
Said Bruce to his companion.
"The great Rabbi Zwi said it best. 'Bruce,' he said... he gave me the nom de plume, Bruce.
'Pour over words which trouble you most; within your colossal view, fuel your lyceum.'"

Teddy stopped in his tracks as he came face to face with a loud, fantastical music hall,
And glancing about the room, he spied bones on the walls near sewer gators in jitter-bug:
"'Self-proclaimed probity, Bruce,' he said; 'be wary of such verbose hyenas,' said Rebbe Zwi.
'Bruce,' he said, Bruce, my name, 'they'll steal the truth away,' say...   See that fella's mug?"
Said the Golem, pointing to red, wiry, grotesque figure pounding on kettles.
"That there, Teddy, sits Amalek himself, Drum Meister... watch your blood does not spurt,"
Said Gretel, just as Ketzele spoke with a hiss.
"He's swishing his finger like I swish my tail. Amateur! Shall he show his middling cat pose?
He swishes us to that odd looking platform, see the elevator sign... My, he's awfully curt."

With Teddy in the lead, the quartet stepped on to the 'elevator' as persuasively suggested,
And a sextet of rats rushed in, shaking its sides, the lead rat spitting out elevator sounds:
"Ding! (said a rat) Bottom floor! Exit wisely, watch the doors, welcome to what's beneath it all.
"Wall mummies are for show, so hug them gently; they severely lack in what you call pounds,"
Noted the lead rat, lugging a tiny saxophone.
"Ladies and Gentlemen! Gators and Slugs! Wave your beanies! Startle awake hanging bats."
Said Amalek to a cheering crowd of those rarely seen.
In association with the Walk the Other Way Rodent Society, direct from the South Side Dump,
And held over lest the slayer arrives, please welcome 'Seymour Rumps and the Sewer Rats!'"

The sextet jumped upon a plywood sheet, the lead rat, Seymour, catching a splinter in his paw,
And dozens of gators in zoot suits bopped heads to rat riffs; the band had the right chops:
"Welcome, arachnids! Welcome all to Nut House, home picked by the dispossessed since 1941.
Welcome Golem! Welcome Cat! Welcome Baker... ah, Gretel, their faces new measures of gawps,"
Snickered Amalek, signaling they should leave the elevator.
"Miss Gretel, how is that you know this jaded fellow? Certainly, he's not a regular diner patron,"
Asked Teddy, his hair caught in one of the hanging webs.
"I've goose pimples rising, Miss Gretel. I feel there might be Amalek's eyes spying right at me.
Oh, I am certain Amalek sets eight eyes upon me. Might I shield myself with your apron?"

Cued, The Sewer Rats launched into one of their popular torch songs, 'One for the Gutter,'
And played tranquil tones, Seymour on sax, four rats accompanying with rattling chains:

> "Never listened to Mother.
> This she said so,
> One for the gutter.
> We've got the vermin blues.
> Purveyors of puss,
> Everywhere we disgust.
> Why, oh, why such distrust?
> We're akin of Cain's..."

Moaned Seymour in piercing crescendo, the band moaning too.

> "Never loved in people light,
> This she said, too,
> One for the gutter.
> We've got the vermin blues."

Rattled on the band leader.

> "Who pities the pests?
> Do we resemble Grendel?
> Who hugs the bugs?
> Oh, to be transcendental.
> Edgar Allan died here.
> Odd Edgar died here.
> One for the gutter.
> Leaving town in vermin shoes."

XI

Amalek launched into a spirited solo, slapping at snares certain they gave him a sneer,
And Teddy noticed a unique rattle to one of the drums, as if a small ball bounced within:
"A Kurt Weill twist: WA! WA! WA! Whiskey! WA! WA! WA! Whiskey, so Seymour goes.
Next Bar.. really uneven bar... WA! WA! WA! Whiskey! WA! WA! WA! Pass the gin,"
Shouted the Sewer Rats, feverously.
"Food for famished fools: I got Texas-sized fangs ready to chew printed decadence like caviar,"
Said Amalek, directly to the baker.
"So scrumptious... to devour what is needed to know... once got Twain stuck between incisors.
AH! Call the dentist! Huck Finn hanging apart... 'ne'er shall the twain meet' Hearty! Har! Har!"

XII

The Sewer rats sang softly under Amalek's monologue, adding layers of nonsense to the night,
And Amalek leaned from his kit, nibbled at a volume of *Ulysses*, mumbled about trials:

> "One gutter
> One for...
> One for the gutter.

Nothing but...
Nothing but strife in these vermin shoes.
Shu... Shu...
Shush the voice
Da... Da...
Damn their choice.
Ver... Ver...
Vermin shoes,
Such crooked miles,"

Sang the harmonic rats, their last words a loud acapella.
"Hooves Horrors! Even a devil needs a little fiber, these days. Care for a little Shakespeare?"
Said Amalek, licking his fingers.
"Shakespeare I gnaw... Marlowe I munch. Shakespeare, my breakfast, a little, Har, 'Hamlet.'
Rooting out whatever vibes we dislike, I devour, gobble... oh you seem despondent, I fear."

XIII

Teddy stepped closer to the demon's drum, passing by chewed pages with names like Douglass,
And the baker, peering into percussion ensemble, realized why it hammered an excitable beat:
"Gretel, Cat, Golem... Odd though it may be, the spice we seek sits encased in Amalek's drum.
I see it by its brilliant glow, how it shines. With such luminosity, it must certainly be sweet,"
Said Teddy, eyeing a bulb bouncing under the drum skins.
"Mr. Baker Man, I'd say bake me cake, but as fast as you might. We've got spoils to delight."
Said Amalek to Teddy, stunned the demon knew his profession.
"Take a crack at our Wacky Cake, DC Hooverville, 1930... rock hard, it's got a noble crunch.
Then, stab at our Boiled Cake. It's got cloves, made with sordid wheat grown in the '31 blight."

Amalek viscously slapped at his kit with the humerus bones of a 19th century timpani player,

And as bones will be bones, one humerus cued the other to regale the guests an insipid yarn:

"Once, a fellow called Max Illa stammered, 'Hot! So Hot! Three centuries under… so hot.

The clay above heats. The clay above presses me. So much clay… I need water in a tricorn,'"

Said the bone, appraising the tale's radius.

"This bag of bones begged for drink, to which neighborly worms said, 'We don't do water,'"

Continued the humerus.

"Yet, he begged and begged for relief. 'Rain! So hot! So Hot!' To which the worms said,

'Fear not this weather; we're under Ohio. It'll change long before lunch. It'll get hotter."

The bones rattled with glee, agreeing callousness must be the way to a gut jiggling guffaw,

And hitting kettle skins, they resolved, these are the things decided under cities at night:

"I find their humor chilling to… well, what an odd place we see all for the want of a spice.

Ketzele, present spears. It's a cat's talons that are most needed for such a situation so tight,"

Said Teddy, determined to grab the bulb and leave, quickly.

"Pierce the kettle, grab the bulb… Oh dear me… to be home to soothe my wife's bunion,"

Said the baker to a cat flashing claws.

"Stifle your fears… be ready to pounce… oh don't worry that Amalek may drink blood.

Ketzele… Don't catch anything, don't kill anything, don't eat anything. Just dig for the Onion."

The Ballad of Golem Bruce

River waves were the kindest of blankets,
A massage – I might say – for my Earthen scalp.
Such pleasure making a Golem somnambulant,
Had this Golem legs while in pleasant sleep.

Now coal barges were the rudest of alarms,
Each blocked – I must say – desired moon glow.
Its insidious racket made this Golem an insomniac,
Proof of worldly cruelty, even to resting clay.

Now, with legs, I trudge away from my river bed,
Limbs pressed together by rabbinical prayer,
A pressed nose – I must say – in need of change,
An extremity – I might say – harshly plucked on.

Do Golems need to smell Resh's treats?
Will Golems even desire Resh's treats?
I shall say so...

Gentle hands shaped me.
Malicious voices now shame me.
Golem obligations press upon me.
Winds slap my earth to break from me.

Do I miss the Scioto muck?
Do I need more Scioto muck?
I shall say so...

Book 4
Scene I
The Science of Pounce

I

Like most war-torn felines, Ketzele proved exacting in her pouncing, crouching, eyeing,
And her tail swishing, well, it must be said her tail swayed with Toscanini-like charisma:
"Um... Ketzele... while it is your systematic approach I appreciate, opportunity departs.
Um Ketzele, please pounce... oh I should have stayed in synagogue, arguing the Mishnah,"
Said Teddy, seeing Amalek munching up Marlowe.
"Bring more of the iambic verse for lunch. Though I fear spondee inspires a toothache,"
Said Amalek devouring more pages.
"I see we got Steinbeck for dessert... love those angry grapes... I like my tortillas flat.
NUM! NUM! Dear rats, such delicious words to eliminate, what else did you take?"

II

Turning their attention to the arrival of more rats, Seymour's band stopped playing,
And, each rat carrying a book, eagerly reported to Amalek the deeds of their cartel:
"Last shipment from shelves south of Tallahassee... library stacks officially vacant.
As severe maladies spark our delight, tell us what waits at the bottom of the Endless Well,"
Said a number of the rats.
"For you, we've got F. Scott, Miller's cancer book... Oh, for your private study, Lady Chatterley,"
Continued representatives of the returned mischief.
"We've brought you four squares for days, so tell us what waits at the bottom of the Endless...
Uh... remember to chew novels accused spurious... uh... devour all certainly misread slowly..."

Teddy realized that questions concerning the Endless Well were off the Amalek's table,
And Ketzele, now curious about the Endless Well, crouched in the direction of its gaping hole:
"Old ketchup and vinegar and fries! This is what you think a gator eats? This menu's a croc!
There must be something fleshier coming down river for us, reptiles on the sewer dole,"
Called out a disgruntled zoot suit dancer.
"Come, fella, step by the Well… Here, you can spy all that flows through a pristine underbelly,"
Said Amalek, guiding and pushing the protestor into the Well.
"A menu's a menu. For your friends, surely it will change as the Neil House clock above bends.
For soon: leftover Woolworth cottage cheese, pineapple, assortments of toast and apple jelly."

The remaining sewer gators moved far from Amalek as the rats deposited disdained books,
And the din of actors emanated from a movie palace above, filled the demon's noxious lair:
"Do I hear Joan Crawford? Why do I hear Joan Crawford? I love Joan Crawford.
Her eyes so… so… piercing… Many nights I sneak in to watch by the projector room stair,"
Ruminated Amalek, looking at the abandoned books about him.
"Ugh! More Huck Finn? Are these leftovers from last week or yet another library clear?"
Spouted the demon, starting his usual midday tantrums.
"Ah, the strains of a matinee. Even an insipid demon like me enjoys a grand picture show.
Say, gray cat, how does your back manage such a severe crouch? Does your swaying tail steer?"

Ketzele flashed graying teeth with a voluminous yawn then licked a paw for extra measure,
And she then chose to hiss at Amalek as he seemingly drew far too close to her:
"Demon! I've many lives now passing before me; there's Mama, Grand Mama Great…
Oh, Great Grand Mama… may I knead on your head, demon, scratch your scalp so leather?"
Asked Ketzele, her question normally not asked courteously.
"What? Expose why a demon does demon things? Come watch a gator display his jackknife,"
Replied Amalek, tossing another unfortunate reptile into the Well.
"There you go beneath the concrete bliss, basement dust, gutter bunk, sewer gunk.
Down the gator rolls, where he will land no one ever knows. Such is a singing demon's life."

Teddy stood behind Ketzele, whose fur fluttered in rows as he slightly touched her tail,
And, with enlarged gray eyes, set focus on Amalek's drum, hearing the falling gator jaw:
"Oh, the price of a suit. Oh, the price of wearing green scales. Oh, the price of gravity.
Oh, the friends I may never… oh my, can it be?… By golly, I see Floridaaaaaaaaaaaah,"
Called out the dispatched gator disappearing into oblivion.
"That I eat what one lone person calls wicked leaves me in a state of cerebral emaciation,"
Said Amalek, accompanying himself with a belch.
"Oh, acid reflux… must be the Hemingway. Steinbeck's easier, for he is far more banished.
These days, expelled pages arrive too often… steals me away from any badge of distinction."

Ketzele, recognizing the greatness of the pages being destroyed, stood tall from her crouch,
And, after an exquisite cat stretch, she courageously sat upon Amalek's literary stash:
"Wispy demon, you have demonstrated exhausted standards of how to wallow in crude.
But what of drool? What of puke? Do you even have an inkling of how to make hairball mash?"
Said the cat, pounding Amalek with piercing questions.
"Gato! Neko! Chat! How ever I should address your presence,... you loaf upon my lunch,"
Shouted Amalek at Ketzele, reclining.
"Mouser, if you can call yourself mouser! I've seven rats here for the chase, yet you lounge.
Now stop lapping your rump. Even I find that ghastly. There are better things here to munch."

Ketzele looked over her leg, offered the demon a steady stare, then proceeded to lick again.
And though with demonic briskness, Amalek shook humerus, Ketzele answered by yawning.
"Fine! Gato! Neko! Chat! I've a show for you. Percussion from 'Fanfare for the Common Rat.'
Come! We'll strike the band in modernist fashion – that theme sounding like day dawning,"
Said Amalek, bouncing rat after rat off the kettle recreating the Copland.
Confound it! I've bounced all my rats only to fall one note short! Oh, what price virtuosity?"
Shrieked the demon, starting the Fanfare over.
"Say, I must admit Baker, Gretel... your presence causes me to be a demon in shutters.
I find none more terrifying than you pair. Your eyes seem to pierce through my pomposity."

Amalek bounced Seymour ferociously, catapulting the crooner off the kettle,
And into the Well. Thrilled at his kettle's rattle, the sewer rats followed suit:

"So tiring, performing. I need a ripe glass of Type B Positive. Any positives out there?

Still, there is the matter of the missing note. I know! I know! Gato, you don't give a hoot,"

Said Amalek, sipping a glass of red liquid, fulfilling his Biblical heritage.

"Do you know how hard it is to be a folk tale like demon in modern days, complete with trams?

Said the demon with snarling charisma.

"Someday, I will introduce you to my cousins, Chort, Murmur and, yes, Ed too. Music lovers all.

Still Gato, Chat... whatever I inspire to call you... I need one more note to complete my jams."

X

The demon looked over Ketzele's shoulder, past the baker, shied from eye contact with Bruce,

And then careful study determined he might get two notes out of Gretel, in with one bounce:.

"Gretel, the rats here have long boasted of nibbling on your stock. Your ears must burn eternally.

Mămăligă! They love polenta, as there's polenta for everybody. Ah, Cat preparing to pounce?"

Said Amalek to the crouching gray hair.

"Just sharpening the old hunting skills, from days when I may have tracked a zebra or two,"

Said Ketzele, once again eying the bulb in the Kettle.

"Pay no attention to my intention, book eater. You need regard the grace of my buttock wiggle.

The worth of a wiggle should not be overlooked, demon. It's not something to misconstrue."

XI

As cats purr truth, Ketzele's backend swayed right to left, then appropriately to the opposite,

Her crouch so brilliantly proficient, it's now (she notes) practiced by every feline in Europa:

"This posture, complicated as it appears, gives fire to my engine, steam propulsion to my hinds.

My leaps? Well, certainly inspired by Fonteyn. My sways... proof I may be a feline Pavlova,"
Said Ketzele, knocking Humerus off the kettle.
"Sounds like dramatic Chat business. What dramatic springs you appear to have, gray puff,"
Said Amalek, chewing on a choice Joyce passage.
Oh, such a canard... sweet, slandered volumes... A glass of vintage blood to wash it all down.
Gretel! You are the missing note. Come be bounced musically, though it'll be a little rough."

XII

Amalek dragged towards the waitress while whiskers, paws, rat noses peered from the Well,
And Rump's Rats held Bruce & Teddy frozen prisoners with forceful off-pitch singing:
"These beautiful rats... they're cool cats with needy chops... they're never late to lunch.
This cat will have her mew. It's an odd day for reflection, say, demon drummer dreaming,"
Mused Amalek, ready to reach for Gretel.
"Say, verse gobbler! Might that be a rare onion rolling about in your vibrating kettle?"
Said Ketzele, in position to finally pounce.
"Excuse me! I need adjust my pupils to thin moons. Butt wiggle! Contact!
Ketzele spears ready.
One last favor, censor head. Give the drum a bit of motion... please, leave free poor Gretel."

XIII

Amalek did as purrs requested, moving the drum teasingly. After twelve stanzas, Ketzele leapt,
And she bounced off toms, catapulted across the room, her fur tickling dangling ceiling pedes:
"Oh, the right drum I missed... excuse me bony toes... ouch, ankle... pardon me stalagmite feet.
Even a harsh army cat like me wears a soft coat... certainly a shock to your frozen heads,"
She said to the feet, her fur not causing shrieks, but sighs.

"You spy my onion, Chat? I've an onion in my kettle... every kettle ought to have an onion,"
Said Amalek to high flying feline.
"What kettle can brew gastric miracles without a singular onion, I ask you, attending chefs?
When cut, more than just tears flow as eyes gaze upon such an aromatic, brilliant bunion."

XIV

Teddy watched the rattling kettle, holding the cure for the Parsons Avenue scarlatina,
And yet it occurred to him: this Onion need be captured then peeled, layered to the core:
"The light you seek, Baker, brims within the bulb your eye desires like an iced cake.
The remedy you seek flourishes only within, never to be found in any apothecary store,"
Said Amalek, reaching to beat humerus once again.
"The trick shall be in retrieving a light so bright, you'll be needing a wide brimmed hat,"
Said the demon, beating the dead timpanist's assailed bone.
"What-ho, devil wannabe! As distinguished captain of Eisenhower's European beach brigade,
Mine ears twitch in much noise from all directions... Dare you call me as a wide room cat?"

XV

So came Ketzele's voice preparing, limb to tail, to pounce the kettle, her buttocks at steady sway,
And Amalek, aware of his weak flank, started a hullabaloo while a turtle dove sang from above:
"Seymour Rump! Rile up the band! Grab Chef Gretel! Toss her by neck into the Endless Well.
Back to your river, Golem! To the barracks, Captain Chat! Somebody stifle that cooing dove,"
Ordered the demon, picking at a nostril with humerus' tip.
"Farbisene! It's a patsh is what you need! A tremendous patsh from my Golem right hand,"

Shouted Bruce at the demon, though feeling hopeless as Gretel flew towards the Well.
"AYE! Old chefs need not fly! Toss me away, devil, if you must. I'm still the superior cook.
Though this toss means doom, it's done wonders for the neck... who shouts 'Huzzah' so grand."

Book 4
Scene 2
A Baker's Tort

I

Quicker than a page turn; Jody's insect consortium constructed a cover over the infamous Well,
And his chainmail of ants caught Gretel supporting her weight of seasoned skin and bone:
"Confound it! Every time I conceive of something awful, I fail. Oh, Seymour, we've ants again.
Humerus, pound me melancholy beats while I hang my head for another opportunity blown,"
Groused Amalek, losing sight of the coveted bulb.
"Oysvorf or Orloff... however they mispronounced your name, your Harbor Island arrival,"
Said Amalek looking up and dropping humerus once upon the kettle.
Rather than Chat's pounce... Rather than Chat's needle-like kneading... try a test, Baker, a test.
Gather together your Shtetl lines, genius. Muster up whatever they cooked up for their survival."

II

Gretel bounced off the ant shield but not before she complimented Jody's tactical craftsmanship,
And like a Chagall angel, she flew into Bruce's arms, a flight correcting her neck's severe crook:
"I have walked a crooked mile or two, earth beast; your catch's as graceful as Joe DiMaggio.
I'm ready for the ground now, Bruce! I'm ready to step with pluck, a little daring-do! Look,"
Said Gretel, her head high for the first time since her windows were shattered in '38.
"Saved you from a plotz. You're the first one I've saved, Gretel, my first and very finest save,"
Said the Golem, attempting a smile but loosing crust in the process.
"Days I wished to save; a Golem's curse is to protect, so said my father, my shaper, Rebbe Zvi.

But, how to protect when an ocean might shed a Golem's hide. This save fits a Golem's slate."

III

Jody gave thought to the Well's lowest stones, then called the able column to attention,
And, recognizing that a descent would require courage, he relied on colony-wide Chutzpah:
"This here's my right hands man, M. Gore-ki, a specialist in taking the next depth lower.
This where we part, gentle Gretel. I look forward to future matzah balls! Troops! Huzzah!"
Called out Jody to his ants, and all disappeared into the Well, Gore-ki on point.
"The Bulb! The Bulb! Mr. Baker wants the Bulb. To win what's within the Kettle, eh?"
Shouted Amalek, feeling ignored as a long series of goodbyes transpired.
"I offer the Bulb should you accurately, Mr. Baker, without hitch nor misguided glitch,
List, in proper order, the process of preparing three delicacies, start to finish, each you'll say…"

IV

Ketzele's back hairs rose straight as Bruce and Gretel prepared for Amalek's worst,
And Teddy quivered, for he hated tests, whether with or without studious cue cards:
"All right, demon with drumstick bones. I accept (gulp), but what might be the consequences,
Amalek? What is that we surrender, should I botch a demon's idea of a delicacy in lard?"
"Consequences? A flavored word. I shall add bitters to the bon mot to encourage my profit,"
Said the demon in stark tone.
"Indeed, I'm in need of new sticks in which to pound banal beats from my kit to the city.
As Le Chat slapped away my symphonic bones, it's your Humerus & Bulb you shall forfeit."

Teddy glanced at his friends, took a deep breath, felt new heat, rubbed his baking arms,
And, looking squarely at the Bulb, he asked Amalek to begin the demon's recipe test:
"Ask your worst, devil face, yet keep your efforts sincere, scrupulous, especially frum.
Whether ginger or honey, poppy or prune, I address your cooking quizzes with my very best,"
Said Teddy, standing with Gretel, Bruce & Ketzele close by.
"Mine eyes primed to create cream horns delicious enough to knock down Jericho's Walls,"
Boasted Teddy, with his trio uncertain whether to cheer or hide.
"Care to start with a good Babka, for in Babka goes all that is good in this world, with raisins.
Please! Your first quiz. I shall not sleep… nor the Golem, Gretel, nor Ketzele sleep. Don't stall."

Amalek beckoned Seymour to produce a banned cookbook that had the whole sewer in stitches,
And Rump produced one that misspelled the Thai word for pumpkin in nervy letters red:
"Ha! International cooking! Here's a favorite – fuk tong! Pumpkin! Oh, the hilarity of immaturity. But seriousness stills my guffaw! Quick, Baker, how to prepare the perfect Mandelbrot Bread?"
Said Amalek, wiping tears from each of his six eyes.
"So almond bread's your first challenge, a delightful choice in much need of chocolate slices,"
Said Teddy, spotting a mourning dove settling on a stone façade just behind Amalek.
"We'll need two oven visits, so gather in cups: sugar, melted butter, flour, that one in three.
Pour in vanilla – portions not voluminous – almond extract, a salt smidge, see how it entices?"

Teddy wiped sweat from his brow, knowing vocalized his recipe completely out of order,
And, yet, he grew more confident discovering that from Amalek's chops flowed drool:
"Ah... um.... Certainly, eggs are the miracle element for any brew, and here we need but a few.
Gather two (the dove cooed thrice) eh... ur... gather three eggs for proper Mandlbroyt fuel,"
Said Teddy, pulling on his collar in order to breathe a little.
"Set your oven at an exacting temperature, for overbaked Mandlbroyt is something to rue,"
Continued the baker, seeing the Golem mouth the words 'chocolate'.
So, with baking powder, chocolate slices, whisk altogether in a favored... um whisking bowl.
Round into a glowing ball, chill for three (dove cooed twice) um.. chill for hours marked two."

The Golem obsessed over the word chocolate, mouthing hard consonants as if each were a bite,
And Ketzele, settled upon his head, enjoyed the gentle ride offered by the Golem's rhythmic jaw:
"So, knead the dough because we need the dough... Ha! Uh... bake for twenty, just twenty.
Lower the heat... we really need to lower the heat, bake for another fifteen. No one like it raw,"
Snickered Teddy, wishing he were back at Herr Resch's bakery demonstrating cream horns.
"Well, upon a greased pan, bake the final bake (the dove cooed thrice)... lest, there be one more."
Corrected Teddy, tipping his fedora to the dove.
"Wait for the golden moment to arrive. Ha! Cool! Oven trips made thrice thus... uh... voila.
Cool! The cooler the cookie the grander the crunch. Devour with awe, after a gentle milk pour."

Teddy smiled, Ketzele stretched, Gretel shined as Bruce considered the texture of chocolate,
And, while strains of Mozart filled the room, Amalek, stomach growling, drooled in gobs:
"Mozart makes me meek… Weak in the knees… Singing 'Flute' keeps the indigestion away
When the two birds, yes those two little birds finally marry, it leaves me in stormy sobs,"
Confessed Amalek, flinging goop straight into Seymour's face.
"Baker! You forget! Portion the bread – I'll show such slices when retrieving your humerus,"
Threatened the dithering demon.
"Yet, sounding somehow awkward, it appears to be a bread I would devour without hesitation.
So then tell me, Baker, what is proper way to make Beetroot Kvass, serving the numerous?"

A 'Magic Flute' aria drifted within, a song where a bird hopes to find a special bird to love,
And as the mourning dove cooed, Teddy carefully considered a recipe he rarely prepared:
"There's a tonic… one calling for a touch of this, a tad of that, achieving a discreet boozy beet.
Wash your beets like you watch your beats, Amalek. Ready to jar your beets… my order erred,"
Said Teddy, joined by singing slugs crooning odes to Kvass.
"Dice them but, good sir, do not dice me. Brine them but do not assault me, dear demon, please,"
Said Teddy, with approval from the dove.
'Wait as you would have waited for almond bread. Within a week, you'll be able sip sneak daily.
Then, sauced, you'll haunt with Amalek gusto from a beverage these blotted slugs might seize."

Amalek, enthused by the prospect of such purple elixir, snarled, then thrashed at the baker,
And with the longest of claws, the demon slashed Teddy's arm, shredding flesh and coat:
"Argh! Amalek! Watch with the finger spikes. Had you useful stuff, I would sue you for tort.
My arm sheds blood! I've delivered recipes to satisfy even you... you pompous shoat... "
Said Teddy, impressing Amalek.
"Fine, Baker, fine. No need to pull barristers into the sewer. Therefore, we'll skip all tortes,"
Retorted the demon.
"Mandelbrot, Kvass aside... explain: cream horns, Baker. Be precise for the right flakiness."
Custard impresses, yet keep the filling light. It is with this recipe your Fate courts."

Teddy pictured his cue cards. Within the recipe he saw Lila, his five babka babies,
And with explosive expertise, he rattled the journey from mixing bowl to divine flakiness:
"Mixing this horned brew, what song then do you sing, Baker? What tune floods your brain?"
What melodies do you croon to the heavens, Baker, to bequeath your crust ideal daintiness?"
Asked the demon, breaking out in a monstrous sweat.
"I sing 'Joshua fought the battle of Jericho! Jericho! Jericho!... you know? you know?"
Said Teddy, with Gretel tending to his wounds.
"Joshua fought the battle of Jericho... uh.. and the walls came tumbling down.
Hum Hāvā Nāgīlā, 'Let us Rejoice,' then tease kindly the jumble into a tubular dough."

As the baker began to recommend a concoction of cream cheese, lemon juice, sugar,
And, instruments of blending, Ketzele made her way towards the Bulb & kettle:
"So then, 400 degrees, nothing less, nothing more, Butter wisely your cooling shells.
Stuff the cream, for what's inside remains the best, its sweetness giving us our mettle,"
Said Teddy, as Ketzele pounced upon Amalek.
"Oh, horrific cold paw pads! I've trapped by cattiness virtuoso! Oh, Joan! Help Me, dear Joan,"
Called out the demon in despair.
"Off tainted Chat! Get thee to a kennel! I scorn your furry companion! Oh, I've lost my curse list.What have I stepped in... brown stone so soft? Argh! Chat! A gifted hairball I thought a stone."

Above Amalek's head, a tremendous shout shook the sewer's foundations, bricks splitting,
And, as some fell upon the demon's many toes, a familiar cry lightened the quartet's hearts:
"Balugaaaaa! Sign me up for those horns! Balugaaaaa! Here's my gracious girth put to the test.
Illuminating needles, I have many from the Rose. I stab thee in your polemical parts,"
Exploded the voice of Burble Friedel, his enlarged hands holding rose thorns.
"Here, demon, have a rose thorn to the thigh. Oh, you've six? A thorn in each, I affix."
Said Burble, flying off as fast as he entered.
"Make the gashes upon the beast severe... greater light shall emanate from bloodied holes.
Go, embattled quartet. The Bulb shall be yours, the Great Onion, should you brave the risks."

Burble out sight, Teddy drew Amalek's attention with recipes as Gretel grabbed up thorns,
And Bruce, ready to punch in the demon's nose, found two to punch, so he punched twice:
"Have a thorn in every one of your sides, you scene chewer you! A thorn by any name still jabs.
OOF! I stab! OOF! Jab a cake... maybe it's done. Jab a demon! Please be gone... Jab trice,"
Said Gretel, stabbing at what she could reach.
"Hush, Slugs! I came from shadowed depths to declare this here my city sewer suzerainty,"
Said Amalek, quieting singing gastropods while engaging Ketzele in a staring contest.
"Ouch! Gretel! Your jabs cause more pain than my stomachs filled with your pot roast.
We are face to face, Chat, the Bulb between us! As for your hiss... it's far too flaunty."

Book 4
Scene 3
Fanfare for the Common Latke

I

Amalek blinked first. His head ached from Golem's fisticuffs, his legs bludgeoned by thorns,
And Ketzele, claws at the ready, slashed into the Kettle drum, scraping the first onion layer:
"Argh! Mine lids hath fluttered. Ugh! Mine noses shattered by paws! Ouch, Gretel.
Methinks I chewed my last decadent tome. Chat, you triumph... an Amalek slayer,"
Cried the demon... his body deflating.
"Bulb seekers! For mine finale... mine dandy exit from this sewer's decaying roof,"
Said Amalek, crawling away from the kettle.
"Though dusty as it may seem, I sweep out of here as do all unappreciated guests.
I must do what an Amalek must do when definitively doomed. Watch me poof!"

II

In an instant, Amalek transformed into plain white moth, flittering in dim light,
And while rising toward the sewer's ceiling, the dove, by beak, snapped him up:
"Light, fare thee well. Evenings chewing Modernists, Au Revoir! Oh, Joyce in Boston.
I must say mine time as a moth... quite dusty... oh, Dove your dining I do disrupt,"
Said the moth, tucked in a bird's mouth.
"I go, Chat, but cry that those in planes and wild cars shall never believe I did tarry,"
Lamented Amalek, within the darkness of a dove's throat.
"I go, Baker, take the Bulb for what it's worth... cure your Babka Babies from the scourge.
Swallow me you must, Dove; remember I'll come out in the end... the very end.... the very..."

III

The quartet could no longer see the demon. Rats along with slugs vanished from the sewer,
And Amalek's voice faded cynically: "All is Bobamayse!" He said. "All is Bobamayse!
Scratch away the layers to find its special light, Captain Ketzele. Give it a good rip & tear.
What joy! I've glee! Bogart shall play my life's story, in Bogie baritone, to be precise,"
Said the Golem, imagining a role for Bergman too.
"Take the Bulb now, Herr Baker; the captain has chewed through. May your latkes be the cure,"
Said Gretel, tossing away a few remaining thorns.
"I've need for the surface; I've need for cold Ohio air. Richard will be by. Richard with a ride.
Herr Baker, Herr Golem & Ketzele… let us once again see skies these ceilings rudely obscure."

IV

Gray had covered the city skies, quite the same as it had been since Teddy's morning study,
And as he pocketed the Great Onion, Ketzele sniffed his fingers with approval; Bruce cried:
"Here's Richard's sled once again… farewell brothers… Steuermann! Find me a better river.
Purr everlasting, Ketzele! Golem! Herr Baker! We glide, graying ice day's ending ride,"
Said Gretel, heading to her vacant café – her neck forever sore.
"Mr. Baker, does your pocket warm from the Great Onion? I sense a glow about you, Maestro,"
Said Bruce, following a moment's reflection for Gretel.
"It's my heart that warms, gentle Golem. I anxiously await a return, with the right Latke spice.
 Potatoes grated… oil at just the right heat… orchestra horns blasting for latkes avec gusto."

V

Three sapped onion seekers stared at a basketweave, colorful ice swirls made by car & wind,
And into the mist, each realized grand designs, which to Teddy suggested a marvelous ganache:
"How does dirty ice cause the stomach to grumble; do I stand before a whipped chocolate sea?
Imagine, Ketzele... oceans of chocolate eddying from sewer to alley – a Ketzele dream nosh,"
Said a drooling Golem, causing a bit of his lip to erode.
"Baker, this is where we part... you to your babkas... Ketzele and I to our placid brick alley,"
Said Bruce, hoping that tears would not erode him further.
"Our risk now over, we need new trades, Ketzele... shall Golem become a ranging ragpicker, Accompanied by cat selling saucers to Parsons Avenue wives... or blue strains of challis?"

VI

Bruce, accompanied by Ketzele, walked straight back to the alley without a glance to Teddy,
And the Golem sat with his back to a stone wall, Ketzele curled upon him like a fur ball kippot:
"Ketzele, how is that cows leap nightly over the moon but by day, they plotz & never fly?
Ketzele, when cows come home, what of their shoes, or what's saved in a bovine's throat?"
Said Bruce, eyes slowly closing.
"Allow my stretching thoughts, Golem... a giant yawn! Now why fiddle with such query,"
Replied Ketzele, reorganizing her curl upon the Golem's head.
"Where do they keep their cud? Why, a cud container in a cud cabinet within the cud closet.
As for flying cows, they do so to tunes by feline virtuosos. Now, sleep; surely you must be weary."

VII

Happy with Ketzele's professorial answer, the Golem closed his eyes to the alley world,

And as luck would have it, Bruce's eyes opened, giving Golem existentialism another glance:
"Ketzele... Do you suppose Jody, with his column, left Amalek's lair to meet Solomon himself?
Ketzele... would a march into the Valley of Ants lead to numerous ants in Solomon's pants?"
Said the Golem, most concerned for the revered King.
"Golem friend, Bruce! The wisest of kings had 900 wives, whereas I've only nine lives on loan,"
Replied the squinting cat.
"Yet, I've fancies as golden as the king. With 900 wives, certainly Solomon's cuffs were sown
As close-knit as wives will sew bonds. Ergo, Golem, ants will never cause the King to groan."

VIII

Once again, happy with Ketzele's reasoned response, Bruce managed to close just one eye,
And sitting quietly for an hour or two, the Golem manufactured a thousand new qualms:
"Ketzele! Ketzele! Ketzele! Where do those living in glass houses change daily underwear?
"Ketzele! Where do Mozart notes go once Mozart tunes stop, and what do you think of Brahms?
Shouted the Golem to his leaping companion.
"Oh... the changing of undies... one should change their drawers while sitting within drawers,"
Said Ketzele, as matter of fact.
Mozart notes hang in skies, clouds, er, forever always kindly floating down for inviting ears.
As for Brahms... well... sleep, Golem. Friend, sleep... relish slumber, relish melodic snores."

IX

Bruce yawned. Ketzele yawned. Grayness brought the impression of dusk. The ice hardened,
And wrapping the cat's tail around his nose, the Golem worried about his Earthen condition:

"Ketzele? Awake now, Ketzele? I worry, Ketzele... how the Earth spins so fast, making days.
How can a figure of clay keep pace with Earth's spins without being knocked into perdition?"
Said the Golem, with a finally warmed nose.
"Truth, Bruce! Nostalgic Mensch! The fastest moving Earth is the marl encasing your heart,"
Said Ketzele, with eyes boring into his alley-mate.
"Hardly can one find a muscle that pounds heavier for his sphere mates... hence fast Earth.
But I have to ask you... wistful lump of clay... within our tight alley quarters... did you fart?"

X

Teddy stood within his Parsons Avenue door, his back to a bowl of finely grated potatoes,
And reaching into his pocket, he found – instead of a special Bulb – a set of finely written cards.
"A song for cakes, Teddy... a song about your baked horns... "Joshua fought the battle...
Teddy, does the ice amaze you? Such a storm... like Passover hail. At what do you stare so hard?
Asked Lila, polishing a bent spoon.
"The many plucked gray hairs I find on the collar of my coat. An afternoon with a... Ketzele... "
Said Teddy, pupils widened like an alarmed cat.
"Ketzele? We've not a cat. Teddy the many gray hairs are yours. You match Ohio's daily sky.
Let's dice the onions... Will our lights burn on for eight days... that storm does bedazzle."

XI

Running fingers across well-read books resting on a shelf, Teddy thought of Amalek's appetite,
And as he stroked sown spines of aged volumes, he mumbled: "Banned! Banned Wanna-Be.
Which pages should I digest, protect by memory, hide their essence from old Amalek?

So nu all my pretty babka babies... Lucia, Mar, Gin, Dorr, Jerzy, beautiful as always, I see,"
Said Teddy, spying small figures peering out a bedroom door.
"When you wander out, do not forget your hat... even if it messes your hair... wear the fedora,"
Said Lila sternly as she placed dishes on the table.
"Wash each hand under the warmest of waters, for soon they will freeze under quarantine order.
Honor thy wife, wear your hat as she wishes. This should be a top command from the Torah."

XII

The children quickly disappeared behind the door, waiting to hear oil sizzle in clad-iron skillet,
And, taking his seat, Teddy studied ancient words for the proper way to prepare Mandlbroyt:
"Twice baked! I am thinking there is more twice baked here than Bubbe's beatific almond bread.
Apologies, Amalek! I misspoke the royal treat recipe, a tall order for a cookie from Detroit,"
Mused the baker, elbows upon the table.
"We've bowls aplenty... borscht to devour... we've ... eat... lest it finally ferment into Kvass,"
Announced Lila to her husband.
"Be sure to eat each and every drop! Loosen the belt, dab in sour cream. Feel fine to slurp.
You've another night with the Maccabees, Herr Baker... you've caring voices to harass..."

XIII

Dropping his cue cards, the cream horn recipe cascading to the floor, Teddy's eyes grew large,
And, though he believed this long day had exhausted him, he actually saw Gretel by the door:
"Eat your borscht, Herr Baker, celebrate your seat by your Babka Babies... apple sauce...
Herr Baker... the layers are shed... you have made it to the core... munch latkes galore,"
Came Gretel's faint voice.

"Gretel, your ride with Richard is complete, no? To which river did you glide?
Is there warmth?"
Said Teddy to the apparent specter.
"Yes... think of all things marvelous that arise from a simple bowl of potatoes
lovingly mashed.
But... Gretel... tell me for certain... I must know... was it for you the dove
cooed... mourned?"

XIV

No answer came from the café entrepreneur. Instead, she shook until she
faded from the room,
And Teddy, snorting, heard his name called, then lifted his arms into a
gargantuan stretch:
"Teddy, you've drooled all about your apron. Certainly, my potato pancakes
are magnificent,"
Say, the ice pounds. Wear your hat... your hair... hair you have none. So why
kvetch,"
Quipped Lila, twirling her spatula.
"Patience! Golden latkes arrive when sunlight retires... horns announcing
their rise from oil,"
Continued the busied chef.
"There'll be a fanfare rousing as Maestro Copland's. Now go... off to Resch's,
the quarantine!
Out! Baker! Knead magically! I'll freshen the borscht... these hours, I've
shaggy beets to boil."

XV

Teddy reached the street, peered but saw no signs of a Golem or even a
brave, gray feline,
And, slipping on the ice, he skated furiously past a mailbox brimming with
buzzard babies:
"It's these daily oddities... Oy... they seem to appear more and in bizarrely
greater doses.
More strangeness to come? Soon, I'll find myself in a boat of imps, paddling
up the Euphrates."
Marveled the baker, rounding the last corner before reaching Resch's.
"Oh, cream horns... how to find its perfection... Joshua... Jericho...
perfection... such cattiness,"
Said Teddy at Resch's door.

"Would it not be a marvel... a melodic dove, bakery-based, providing precise recipes by coo.
Oh, such would be a cream horn's dream... perhaps more a brainy film of a baker's flakiness."

Les Epstein is a poet, playwright, opera librettist and educator. His work has appeared in journals in the United States, Philippines, India, Canada, Ireland and the UK, including Slant, Muse McMaster, The Bacopa Review, The Clinch Mountain Review and Empyrean as well as the anthologies Heat the Grease (Gnashing Teeth Publishing) and Pain & Renewal (Vita Brevis Press). He is the author of Sleep Cinematic: a Golem's Quartet (Gnashing Teeth) and Kip Divided (Finishing Line Press). As a playwright, his work has been staged by such theaters as The Belfast Maskers (Maine), Greenbriar Valley Theater (West Virginia), Stone's Throw Dinner Theater (Missouri) and the Roy Arias Studio